PRAISE FOR
THE UNSTOPPABLE FRANCHISEE

"*The Unstoppable Franchisee* is informative, engaging, well written, and deserves to be read by everyone with an interest in the franchise community."

GRAHAM COOKE, vice president of new restaurant expansion, A&W

"Gary elegantly captures the essence of what it takes to build (or reinvigorate) a strong franchise business. If you are looking for a step-by-step guide to help take your business to the next level, this is it. What's most powerful is that all the steps build upon each other to create an even more valuable playbook."

ALICIA MILLER, co-founder and managing director of Catalyst Insight Group

"*The Unstoppable Franchisee* clarifies and illustrates the interconnectivity and difference in responsibilities between the franchisor and franchisee from both perspectives. Prenevost's work has helped me to identify the key opportunities for my business, which has kept me moving along the right path. I easily related to the different stages of franchise ownership and what I need to do to grow to the next level. Every franchisor and franchisee needs to read this book."

RUSSELL GRANT, Regis Salons multi-unit holder

"It was through Gary's guidance and expertise that I started my journey into franchising. For him to put his knowledge and that of many other industry leaders into one book, well, it's a must-read—you won't regret it!"

COLIN BATES, Jan-Pro regional developer

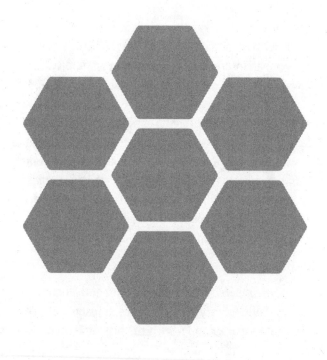

THE
UNSTOPPABLE
FRANCHISEE

7
Drivers of
Next-Level
Growth

GARY PRENEVOST

Vancouver / Toronto / Berkeley

Cataloguing data is available from Library and Archives Canada

ISBN 978-1-77327-191-0 (hbk.)
ISBN 978-1-77327-192-7 (ebook)
ISBN 978-1-77327-193-4 (pdf)

Jacket design by Teresa Bubela and Naomi MacDougall
Front jacket illustration by Teresa Bubela from martialred / stock.adobe.com
Interior design by Jessica Sullivan

Developmental editing by Don Loney
Substantive editing by Steve Cameron
Copy editing by David Marsh
Proofreading by Renate Preuss
Indexing by Stephen Ullstrom

The Alternative Board is trademarked. Used by permission.

Printed and bound in Canada by Friesens
Distributed internationally by Publishers Group West

Figure 1 Publishing Inc.
Vancouver BC Canada
www.figure1publishing.com

Figure 1 Publishing is located in the traditional, unceded territory of the xʷməθkʷəy̓əm (Musqueam), Sḵwx̱wú7mesh (Squamish), and səlilwətaɬ (Tsleil-Waututh) peoples.

TO MY MOM AND DAD:

Through your words and your actions, you taught me strong core values; you also instilled in me an intense determination and will to win. It didn't matter when I got knocked down or fell over; what mattered was that I got back up again and gave it my all, learned from my experiences, and figured out how to improve. When life presented those challenges, you were there to support me as I grew to understand that obstacles were there to learn from, to get over, under, around or through . . . even when they stood between us.

 You would both be described as salt of the earth people—humble and deeply caring. Thank you both for supporting me in my journey to become unstoppable. In the end, all that remains is love.

CONTENTS

PART TWO: The Growth Helix

LIST OF INTERVIEWEES

Colin Bates, regional developer, Jan-Pro of Canada
Doug Brauer, franchisee, FASTSIGNS
Angela Brown, franchisee, Blo Blow Dry Bar
Bob Danielson, former franchisee, FASTSIGNS
Don Elliott, franchisee, Great Clips
Michael Gilpin, franchisee, FASTSIGNS
Sean Hassan, regional developer, Jan-Pro Franchise Development
Cynthia Keenan, franchisee, Blo Blow Dry Bar
Sarosh Nayar, franchisee, FASTSIGNS
Shane Noble, franchisee, Kitchen Tune-Up
Clara Osterhage, franchisee, Great Clips
Sam Reges, franchisee, Great Clips
Jared Rothberger, regional developer, Jan-Pro Franchise Development
Brad Rush, regional developer, Jan-Pro Franchise Development
Heather Stankard, franchisee, Blo Blow Dry Bar
Tom Taube, franchisee, Kitchen Tune-Up
Emily Wilcox, franchisee, Great Clips
Joel Winters, franchisee, Kitchen Tune-Up

FRANCHISOR SENIOR EXECUTIVES
Jania Bailey, CEO, FranNet
Charles Bonfiglio, CEO, Tint World
Stuart Burns, president, SpeedPro Graphics
Adam Contos, former CEO, RE/MAX

Graham Cooke, vice president of new restaurant expansion, A&W
David Druker, president, The UPS Store, Canada
Gary Findley, CEO, Restoration 1
Rob Goggins, CEO, Great Clips
Lane Kofoed, CEO, Assisting Hands
Jack Lapointe, founder, Jan-Pro
Ken LeBlanc, CEO, Property Guys
Ned Lyerly, CEO, CKE Restaurants (Hardee's and Carl's Jr.)
Dan Monaghan, founder, Clear Summit Group
Catherine Monson, CEO of Propelled Brands and past chair
    (Feb. 2020 – Feb. 2022) of International Franchise Association
Heidi Morrissey, president, Kitchen Tune-Up and Bath Tune-Up
Dave Mortensen, president, Anytime Fitness and Self
    Esteem Brands
Doug Phillip, president, Budget Blinds
John Prittie, CEO, Two Men and a Truck Canada
Chris Rondeau, CEO, Planet Fitness
Mark Siebert, CEO, iFranchise Group
Josh Skolnick, co-founder and CEO, HorsePower Brands
Mary Kennedy Thompson, chief operating officer and director
    of Veterans Affairs, Neighborly organization
Steve Thompson, CEO, FocalPoint
Rob Weddle, former CEO, The Cleaning Authority
Graham Weihmiller, chairman and CEO, Business Network
    International
Steve White, president and COO, PuroClean
Vanessa Yakobson, CEO, Blo Blow Dry Bar
Josh York, president and CEO, GYMGUYZ
Jason Zickerman, president and CEO, The Alternative Board

FRANCHISE INDUSTRY EXPERTS
Keith Gerson, president of Franchise Operations, FranConnect
Greg Nathan, psychologist and founder, Franchise Relationships
    Institute
Edith Wiseman, president of FRANdata

INTRODUCTION

MARY KENNEDY THOMPSON, COO of the Neighborly organization, which is the parent company of twenty-nine home service brands in nine countries,[1] offered her insights into why she was attracted to franchising: "I became a franchisee because I wanted to control my own destiny, but I knew I didn't know how to run a business. Operational excellence is something that's always fascinated me. So, give me the system and let me do the absolute best with it I possibly can to operationally execute. For a franchisee, there's a lot of reward in that."

So why is incremental, year-over-year progress towards operational excellence elusive for many franchisees?

- Is it because franchisees are independent business owners who can and do make their own decisions about how to run their business, think they know best for their business, and ignore direction from their franchisor?
- Is it because many franchisees are running "good enough" businesses and don't want to put more effort into their business than they already do?
- Is it because franchisees are focused on coping with advancing technologies and other market changes that are coming fast and hard, influencing their staff, processes, and even their customers' buying behaviors?

1

- Is it because training costs money and franchisees struggle with how long the return on investment takes, or fear that the training might not deliver the results the franchisee is looking for?

This book seeks to answer these questions and others, and to challenge current thinking and assumptions people have about running a franchise. What follows in these pages is the sum of my fact-finding mission on how franchisees can achieve and sustain operational excellence. The seven growth drivers I've identified, if thoughtfully considered and consistently executed, will allow you, as a franchisee, to take your franchise to the next level, and the next, and the next. With this system you can climb as high as your ambition takes you.

Cracking the Franchisee Performance Code

In trying to solve the puzzle of how franchisees might achieve faster next-level growth, and maybe even super-performance, I first started paying attention to things from a 30,000-foot view.

There are thousands of franchise systems in over three hundred different industries. My own experience as a top-performing franchisee (TPF) could not cover the industry span; hence I decided the best way to gather intelligence was to interview franchisees and franchisors across a spectrum of businesses and geographies, and close my knowledge gap by observing and learning the traits and behaviors of top performers. For this exercise I delineated the top 4 percent of franchisees as my differentiating benchmark. This group is the "Pareto's Pareto" of top performers—the 80/20 of the top 20 percent of the franchisee base in their respective systems. They are the super-performers within each franchise brand.

I then began my intensive research interviewing franchisees and franchisors, knowing that I needed to gain insights about operational excellence from several different perspectives:

- from the top 4 percent of franchisees across multiple industries
- from CEOs and COOs of franchise systems across multiple industries

- from franchise industry coaches and thought leaders
- from franchise industry research firms (e.g., the Franchise Relationships Institute, FRANdata, FranConnect)

It wasn't enough to just get perspectives across different industries; I felt it was critically important to also look at different sizes of franchise systems, from emerging fast-growth systems with fewer than one hundred franchisees to franchises with multi-billion-dollar annual sales volumes and thousands of franchisees. I also knew I had to make a point of profiling franchise systems owned by private equity groups, as well as systems that were privately owned by their founders.

Next, I created a set of interview control questions for each group. In addition to exploring what drove top performance, I examined what prevented franchisees from achieving higher levels of success. Then, over the course of nearly eighteen months, I dedicated hundreds of hours to conducting and reviewing interviews with the aforementioned groups. I am very grateful to everyone who contributed.

The findings of my interviews made it clear that top performance is not reserved for those select few who possess a magical blend of personality traits, education, and work history; instead, anyone, regardless of personality type, skillset, market experience, or business background, can and did learn how to achieve top performance. They grew into great business owners over time. To quote author Jim Collins, "Greatness is not a function of circumstance. Greatness, it turns out, is largely a matter of conscious choice."[2]

Collins's book *Good to Great* contains so much wisdom that readers will find something new no matter how well-worn their copy is. The very first words in chapter 1 are "Good is the enemy of great." This holds true in the franchise industry: there are many "good" operators of franchise units, across many systems. They have a good strategy, a good team, a good customer base, and drive good profitability. They are *competent and comfortable* at their current level. While that level of success could not have been reached without the traits and behaviors that created it, living in a kind of business comfort zone is also a barrier to greatness. As you continue to read this book, you will a) be introduced to seven drivers that can grow your business, and b) hear from franchisees and franchisors whose decisions and actions were based on these drivers and led to high performance.

The 7 Growth Drivers

These drivers are a product of my research. They are not drivers I developed in advance as some kind of method and then cherry-picked interview content that fit the method. The drivers are sets of actions taken by franchisees that cumulatively create a roadmap for continuous improvement and growth, regardless of franchise industry, size of market, external market conditions, or size or type of staff. A chapter is devoted to each driver in Part One of the book.

The first driver is about how to grow a next-level mindset—it's the "how" in scaling a business. As Angela Brown, a franchisee of Blo Blow Dry Bar, told me, a lot of growing a next-level mindset "has to do with having a clear vision on where you're trying to get to. I plan for the entire year, and reverse-engineer action steps to get [to my goals]. When you think about being a leader, you must have a vision that's audacious—something that pushes the envelope. If it doesn't scare you, it's not big enough." Angela's words encompass two critical dimensions—operational management and leadership—and we will hear more from Angela on these topics as well as on thought leadership from other franchisees.

The second driver is about growing your awareness. Awareness can include many things, both external (what is going on in your community or region, or beyond, that can affect your business) or internally (such as staff and systems). Sam Reges, a highly successful Great Clips franchisee, talked to me about the consequences of losing awareness:

> I think sometimes people spend so much time worrying about those around them, what I would consider competitors, they sometimes lose focus of what's happening in their own house. I know a

little bit about what's going on with my competitors, but I don't get too worried about that because if I'm doing what I need to do in my house, my competitors aren't going to be of concern. With my staff, my managers, and everybody along the way, we stop worrying about what so-and-so is doing. Focus on yourself and your people, and do not worry so much about what everybody else around you is doing.

Focus on your people

Top-performing franchisees have learned how to master their sense of awareness and keep it acutely tuned to identify opportunities and challenges that they'll encounter in their businesses. You will see how you can immediately begin to apply the practices that TPFs use to leverage their focus, energy, and resources to continually identify, assess, and capitalize on the best opportunities that land on their radar screens.

A next-level mindset and awareness are closely linked. A next-level mindset enables you to decide what goals to pursue; awareness enables you to prioritize where to bring your time, money, and resources to bear—and where and when to reallocate when necessary.

Where to prioritize

The third driver is about improving your operational management skills. My interviewees spoke at length on how they improved customer satisfaction, tightened up their operations, and found efficiencies to reduce costs. Graham Weihmiller, chairman and CEO of Business Network International (BNI), offers this insight:

(3) improve operational mgmt ↓ Focus on execution

> Top performers are really execution focused. Sometimes you have a new franchisee, they want to change the brand overnight. They want to introduce different products or services. Those things may or may not be on the franchisor's roadmap. But the franchisee that is focused on execution of the existing brand is probably going to do better. Now, they should always provide ideas and feedback to the franchisor, and the franchisor ideally is going to involve them in the decision-making process. But I think what is key is that the franchisee understands at any given point, their primary role is the excellent and consistent execution of the existing model.

④
Grow
your
people

The fourth driver is about growing your people. You will hear an emphatic message from the contributors that their team, and not the customer, is their first priority. A team that is committed, energized, and accountable, and is provided with the right training and environment, will thrive. Leaders who live their values and invest in their people can and do scale up their business. The team members develop additional talents, take on more responsibilities, and drive more growth and improvements.

Sam Reges embraces the opportunity to influence her people. In her interview, Sam gave an example of having impact when the perfect candidate is not available.

> It becomes a blessing when you get to take somebody who maybe wasn't the cream of the crop, and you get to really impact them. No matter what level of management you are in, the goal should be to impact the person who needs the most coaching. When we have helped someone, they have said to us, "When I went to school, people told me I was never going to succeed." Seeing these people grow is exciting for me, and I think that if we were in a situation where we could always pick and choose our staff, we might miss out on some of those people who aren't the perfect candidate or aren't as passionate, but engage development.

⑤
MASTER
THE
SYSTEM

The fifth driver is about mastering the system. Catherine Monson, CEO of Propelled Brands and past chair of the International Franchise Association, is among the most respected women in franchising. When I asked her what the most important traits of her top franchisees were, her very first response was the ability to follow the system: "Because I think the vast majority of franchisors have a system. And when it's followed, it's good, it works, and it produces profit for the franchisee."

Joel Winters, a franchisee with Kitchen Tune-Up, agrees, and he questions the mindset of franchisees who think they know better than the system.

People who think, "I already know everything. I don't need the franchise's help." I think that's very detrimental, and I think trying to reinvent pieces of a given franchise model—just because you don't like it or don't particularly adhere to it or understand it—I think that's very dangerous. Most of the time, if you're buying into the right franchise, the model is already perfected and figured out, and clearly people have already made money, have had fun, and have built businesses. I think a lot of times people get into it and try and assert their position and try and reinvent things when it's already been proven to work.

You don't buy a McDonald's and then say, "Well, at Hamburger University, they've got some work to do." It's not right. You wouldn't do that as a brand-new franchisee. You would say, "It's already proven to work. I'm going to take notes. I'm going to follow the process." I think too many people are too quick to say, "This thing is broken and I'm here to fix it." As a business owner, I just think that's the wrong move. I think you need to exploit everything that's already been leveraged for you.

Mastering the system is not just about mastering the basics, though. It's about living and breathing the brand, and about being constantly focused on incrementally improving systems and processes, and being willing to share this knowledge with the franchisor and peer franchisees. Innovation is not removed from this process; it is refined to fit within the system that it benefits.

[handwritten margin note: CONSTANTLY FOCUSED ON IMPROVING SYSTEMS AND SHARE WITH FRANCHISEES]

As you learn how TPFs master their basics, then get to the next level and master the basics there, you'll see that TPFs leverage the collective brain trust of the entire franchise system, part of which is sharing and drawing upon lessons from the successes and failures of other franchisees in the system—at least from those who are willing to share. You will see how and where you can implement some of these strategies in your own business. While this fifth driver may seem similar to the third, "Growing Your Operational Management Skills," it is very different. The third driver is about strengthening your skills; this one is about learning how to execute the business model brilliantly. Developing your skills is just one part of system mastery.

The sixth driver focuses on growing your interdependence, which is the sign of a maturing and successful franchise business. In this chapter, I liken the process to the stages of childhood, teenagerhood, and adulthood. As children depend on parents and family for the necessaries of life and to grow, early-stage franchisees rely heavily on the franchisor to learn how to ramp up their business and achieve stability. Then there comes the time when the business achieves a level of performance where the hard work and the brand have come together.

As teenagers feel and test their independence, so do franchisees once they achieve stability. This independence stage might manifest as "I don't need to follow the system" or "what value am I getting for my royalty dollar" or "I know better than you" or in a myriad of other ways that they start pushing back against the franchisor's model instead of working with it. As they shift from teenager into adult, young adults mature into a state of mutual trust and respect with their parents—a state of interdependence. I discovered that the richest relationships enjoyed by franchisees are a result of evolving from independence to interdependence. I also discovered that many franchisees simply don't evolve to this final stage.

The importance of transitioning from independent to interdependent was one of the major themes that emerged from the research. Without exception, every single top-performing franchisee I interviewed demonstrated and espoused the mindset and all the qualities of having an interdependent relationship with their franchisor.

The evidence of the link between a franchisee's sustained growth and interdependence with their franchisor is undeniable, so in this chapter we'll identify strategies and pathways to help you progress further toward interdependence.

Chris Rondeau, CEO of Planet Fitness, talked about the healthy balance interdependence creates:

In franchises in general, there're always times that franchisees challenge [the franchisor]. Sometimes, that is a good challenge. I think it's unnecessary at times, but franchisees also are sponges in the sense that they want to learn and listen from the franchisor. Not that the franchisor always knows better, but the franchisor has a lot more points of view and a lot more data than individual businesses. We see things geographically and we have just a lot more stuff. The franchisees are willing to learn or willing to get smarter.

The seventh driver is about cultivating a neural network for your business by using Key Performance Indicators (KPIs) and a performance measurement system. It's the old adage that you never know if you've achieved a goal if you can't measure it. The topic of measuring success was a robust part of many of my interviews, though interviewees were unanimous that before anyone can measure success, they have to know what they are aiming at. Every top franchisee is acutely goal-directed, and those goals are aligned with business purpose and values.

Brad Rush, a regional developer at Jan-Pro, offers a list of some of the KPIs that guide the day-to-day activities of his business:
- the number of inspections we do every week
- the number of our account losses for the week
- the number of appointments we set
- the number of proposals we delivered, and the dollar value of those proposals
- the number of accounts we signed
- how much new business we built
- our revenue—how much we've collected

Brad says, "And we have certain percentages that we know we needed to be at during a certain phase of the month. And all those things are measured. So, if we're behind 20 percent in a certain area, everybody knows it. If we're running an excess of 20 percent in a certain area, everybody knows it."

This chapter will provide several strategies that you and your team can utilize to more precisely chart your course, track performance, and make mid-course corrections. Suffice it to say there are many insights in measuring growth and steps to take to fix challenges and knock down barriers to growth.

....

**"Progress is not inevitable.
It's up to us to create it."** ANONYMOUS

....

The Growth Helix

The evidence is that the seven drivers represent the way top performers run their business in order to achieve and exceed their goals. As you progress through the book, you will be given actionable steps you can begin to apply right away to create or accelerate the drivers in your franchise.

Here again are the seven drivers:

1. Grow a Next-Level Mindset
2. Grow Your Awareness
3. Grow Your Operational Management Skills
4. Grow Your People
5. Master the System
6. Grow Your Interdependence
7. Cultivate the Neural Network of Your Business

In Part Two of this book I present you with a new model, unique to the franchise industry, which illustrates how highly successful franchisees scale their business. I call it the Growth Helix. Here's how this concept works: the franchisee learns and masters the basics of the franchisor's system and builds enough business upon that by executing those basics brilliantly, while also experimenting around the edges—succeeding at some things and failing at others, but constantly seeking the lessons of either, and improving incrementally until they're ready to get to the next level of performance

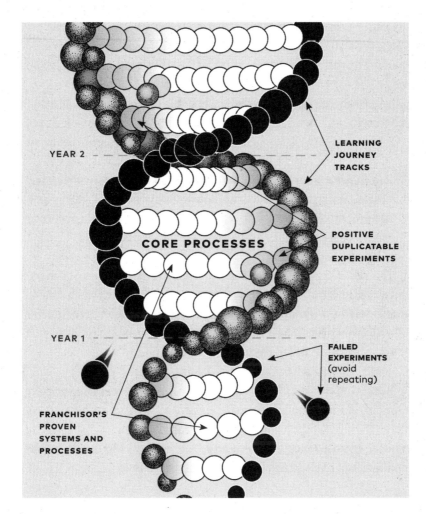

or growth. Then they climb to the next level, and repeat this pattern, then escalate to the next level, repeat again, then climb again—you get the idea. With each new level comes more opportunity and more desired results.

Situation: Franchisee wants to take their business to the next level, and then the next. In other words, continuously evolve and improve the business, and maybe buy more franchises.

Challenge: The franchisee is stuck and it could be because of one or more of the following: they have operational issues; they need to convert more prospects into customers; they need to improve customer experience and grow customer loyalty; they are suffering a lack of leadership skills and are failing staff in terms of growing them and graduating them into roles with higher accountability; they need to get tighter control of costs; etc.

Solution: The Growth Helix is a graphic representation of mindset growth and business growth, achieved by navigating a series of opportunities and challenges that lead to continuous improvement.

- The center column of this image represents the core systems and processes of the franchise model you bought into. Sticking with the processes and working with the franchisor to make improvements are essential to operating a successful franchise.

- The outer rings represent the learning journey, or experimenting around the edges of the core. The light ring represents those incremental changes that make a positive change to efficiencies and productivity, and the dark ring represents those ideas that were tried but failed to improve the business.

Executing the "core" track well ensures you maintain and protect your current levels of performance, while at the same time putting some resources (time, energy, some money if necessary) into the "experimenting" track enables you to explore ways to optimize the business and evolve to your next performance level.

- Core track: This is doing what you know works, every day, every week, every month. It's following the franchisor's business model and executing the core elements to the best of your ability. It's what "got you to here."

- Experimental track: This is what you do once your core track is running smoothly. It's trying new things; it's being curious and testing some of the boundaries of some elements of your core processes to see if there are new or different ways to get better results. A key part of experimenting is keeping detailed notes of the experiments and measuring results.

[handwritten margin note: EXPERIMENT ONLY AFTER CORE TRACK IS RUNNING SMOOTHLY]

Each of the seven drivers is linked to the Growth Helix. The order in which you take on each track depends to a degree on your business and how you have prioritized opportunities and challenges. This can be done by a SWOT analysis: strengths, weaknesses, opportunities, and threats. Regardless of which type of franchise business you're involved in running, I invite you to think about and apply the six-step process outlined below as a way to manage your growth and along the way make incremental changes to your leadership and management skills:

Step 1: Assess the Strength of Your Current Core
Step 2: Identify Possible Growth Areas
Step 3: Plan Your Growth Track
Step 4: Execute Your Growth Plan
Step 5: Measure Progress Regularly
Step 6: Apply Lessons Learned and Make Mid-course Corrections

MANAGE your GROWTH

Moving from new learning to operational efficiency to operational excellence is what these six steps are all about. Once you have reached operational excellence with any new process, congratulations! You've just completed a full cycle for your Growth Helix and you're ready to begin the next one.

The more you practice and apply this six-step growth process, the more it will become comfortable for you. A natural by-product is that you'll be helping your key staff build this critical skillset. The better they learn it, the more responsibility they can take on, which will free up some of your bandwidth to focus on loftier business or personal growth goals.

The Growth Helix is dedicated entirely to enabling you to identify, prioritize, and then build your action plan for the work you'll want to do on your most important opportunities and challenges; Part Two of this book includes a full suite of exercises for you to do to accomplish this. These exercises will also help you to measure your performance for each of the seven drivers and then lay out a plan for overcoming your challenges and pain points.

You might want to complete the work in the Growth Helix progressively from front to back. Or you might prefer to prioritize an area of your business that you know needs work, and use the Growth Helix exercises for that particular driver to drill deeply and thoroughly. The surveys in each of the seven driver chapters are designed to help you assess where you personally are strong and where you need to develop skills; these surveys will also help you to assess where your business is strong and where it is weak.

....

**Garyism: "What do we have to give up
for the time being in order to get started,
or in order to get ahead?"**

....

BEFORE WE DIG IN and get you and your franchise on the path to next-level success, I'd like to start chapter 1 by sharing with you a little learning from my franchisee journey. It is one thing to interview franchisees and franchisors; it's another altogether to live the franchise life day in and day out. It's a life I'm proud to say I love. I wouldn't trade the ups, downs, bumps, scrapes, successes, and failures for anything.

Also let me say that I am immensely grateful to the many top-performing franchisee experts and franchisor CEOs who granted me an interview because they would like to help you get to the next level. Collectively, we have your best interests at heart.

Go to the website theunstoppablefranchisee.com and download the Growth Plan Workbook, which is yours to use to build your own winning action plan. I also urge you to keep a journal as you reflect on the various and instructive experiences you will read about.

PART ONE

THE

DRIVERS

THE STORY BEHIND THE HEXAGON

You might be wondering why I chose a hexagon for the book cover design and chapter theming. Well, the hexagon is one of nature's strongest geometric shapes and represents the most efficient combination of strength and use of space. When built properly and led by people who care about their processes, franchisees, and other stakeholders, the business format franchise is arguably one of the best business models ever invented—the parallels between nature's hexagon and the franchise business model are too powerful to ignore.

A single hexagon is strong; when seven are grouped together a "cell" is formed, where the center hexagon is protected on all sides. As more hexagons are added, each new outer layer adds more strength and protection to the inner layers. An incredibly durable core is created. Does that not describe a successful franchise system?

The franchise owner and the business system form the center hexagon. Combine each franchisee's cell with all of the other franchisee cells in the system and you get a very robust community of like-minded operators. This community forms both a competitive advantage and a competitive protection.

The hexagon model is tied to the seven drivers presented in this book. Each driver is a power-up that strengthens the individual franchise owner, each of their team members, and their overall business. When all seven are cohesively at work, the franchise owner harnesses and directs an unstoppable force.

CHAPTER 1

THE PULL OF ENTREPRENEURSHIP

YOU HAVE PICKED UP THIS BOOK because you are striving to get optimum results in your business, or you're motivated to take on a new business opportunity. So, how can I help you meet your goals and aspirations, or solve your problems and overcome your challenges? Let me begin by sharing a few things about my career and my life in franchising.

I grew up in a large family. My parents instilled in their children the desire and ability to be self-reliant—and hypercompetitive! I'm the middle child among four brothers and one sister. Many "middle child stereotypes" definitely fit me.

I was hyper-energetic, unfocused, always looking for the next opportunity—something more, something better. This became a driving force throughout my career. I had my first paper route when I was six years old. By the time I was thirteen, I had one of the largest *Toronto Star* routes in the city. It took me three hours every day to finish the route.

By the time I was twenty-one I'd gone through the exact same number of different jobs, from short-order cook to dump truck driver to construction worker. I regularly held two or three part-time jobs at the same time. If an employer wouldn't give me enough hours, I'd find another job to fill the time I had available. I was able to develop a wide skill base and became comfortable in working with all types of people and backgrounds. But my education suffered. I lacked the discipline to focus my energy on scholarly pursuits.

I didn't know it at the time, but by having so many jobs so early in life, I discovered which types of work I enjoyed, and which types I would avoid if I could.

I decided that it was time to get serious about having a career, and so I got into the management training stream with one of Canada's big banks. Working at the bank was another cornerstone experience of my career, because I experienced a strong learning culture. I had great management support and was able to develop leadership and interpersonal and business skills, albeit from a conservative banker's perspective. As I progressed, I was given more operational responsibility, eventually overseeing all non-credit (lending) functions of the retail branches I was posted in. I relocated six times in about eight years, with my last two postings being assignments to help turn around underperforming branches.

Even while I had a good job with the bank, I was still seeking additional challenges. While posted at a branch in northern Manitoba, part of the community service I undertook was to become a first responder with the local volunteer ambulance organization. Over the ensuing five years, I would see things and encounter situations that I'd rather forget. People expired in my hands. I loved and hated the work at the same time. Saving someone in distress is a feeling that is hard to describe. Not being able to save someone stays with you and is one of the most difficult stresses to overcome.

If I can boil those five years as a first responder into one statement that might help you to make the right call in going forward in your life, it is this: life is truly a gift and can change in a heartbeat, so live it to the fullest. Plan for tomorrow but live for today, and live each day as if it is your last. Love most of what you're doing, or make a change into something where you can!

Life can be ironic at times. I penned the opening words to this chapter around 6:30 a.m. on Saturday, July 31, 2021. Later that day, my wife and I had a lovely dinner with my dad and mom. We left their house around 9 p.m. Less than two hours later, my dad had a serious accident in his home and was rushed to the hospital; I arrived in time to meet the ambulance. He never regained consciousness and passed away just before 5:30 p.m. the next day. Although we did not know it at the time, July 31 was his last living evening. Life truly can, and did, change in a heartbeat that night for us; we found great peace and comfort in having been able to share his last evening together. As I said, live every day as though it is your last.

While I was learning a ton at the bank, the "love what you're doing" attitude was really weighing on me. I grew unhappy. I was significantly outperforming the previous incumbents of the position, but was getting paid significantly less because I did not have a university degree. I was a strong performer and liked a lot of the work I was doing, but a critical element was missing—the reward was not commensurate with the effort. Also, banking is averse to change. Even when I saw the opportunity to optimize something, the approvals process was stifling.

When I was denied a requested raise, I realized at that moment corporate employment was no longer where I belonged. It was time for me to leave. This was my first experience with a "growth catalyst"—a decision we take, for better or worse, because maintaining the status quo is too painful. A growth catalyst can come in many forms, as you will discover throughout the book.

From Corporate to Entrepreneurship

I did a 180-degree turn after leaving the bank in 1987, taking a 100 percent commission job in life and disability insurance sales with New York Life. In my first month, I earned nine dollars. But in my second month I doubled what I had been earning per month at the bank and never looked back. That was it. I was hooked on self-reliance and working for myself. Thirty-five years later, I still love the autonomy, control, and responsibility—and especially the financial and lifestyle freedom—in working for myself and fulfilling my entrepreneurial spirit.

Since that fateful decision in 1987, I've owned eight different businesses; I guess you can call me a serial entrepreneur. Here's a snapshot.

I've been involved in start-ups, partnerships, and family businesses; bought franchises for myself and brought new franchise concepts to Canada. I even had a five-year run helping companies convert their businesses into a franchise model. I'm now a thirty-year veteran of the franchise industry; I've been on the board of directors for the Canadian Franchise Association for over ten years and am one of Canada's leading authorities on franchising.

My first foray into the franchise industry was with a training company where, over ten years, I awarded sixty-seven of 110 licenses for our new distributors. I also bought a distributor license for myself. Between these overlapping roles, I coached hundreds of entrepreneurs and trained over one thousand salespeople. My most successful business has been my multi-unit FranNet franchise, which I still own and run today. My team and I have helped over two thousand people seriously explore their entrepreneurial options. For most of my twenty-year tenure with FranNet, I've consistently been among their top five franchisees, and even been No. 1 a couple of times.

It hasn't all been roses. I've had painful entrepreneurial experiences, and perhaps this one was the worst. One of the businesses my dad and I bought was a master franchise model for a mobile advertising company that was already in twenty-five countries. In 2005, with my dad's forty years of corporate experience and my growing franchise-industry experience, we bought out the struggling Canadian master franchisee thinking we could turn things around and knock the cover off the ball. Well, we totally misread the opportunity. Over the next three years we kicked, dragged, and clawed our way through every challenge, and there were many; we came to a point in late 2008 where we hit our line in the sand and made the decision to wind down the business—after losing $1.3 million. Fortunately, my FranNet business remained strong and what losses weren't covered by FranNet were incurred by my mom and dad; it took me another five years to repay their losses and make them whole again.

So, if you're still at the business ownership exploration stage, don't make the mistake I did: don't get seduced by an opportunity! That's exactly what my dad and I allowed ourselves to do with the mobile advertising business. With all of my franchise industry experience, I should have known better, but I ignored the logic of the evidence and was seduced by the emotional lure of what we saw as a massive income opportunity.

When investigating business opportunities, whether it is the first step toward launching a new business or taking your existing business to the next level:

1. Investigate every aspect of the business model. While we did extensive research, including talking to existing franchisees and flying overseas and visiting operations, we did not do enough research on how the model would need to be adapted to function in Canada.

2. Understand what type of customers you'll need and want.

3. Understand the work it will take to get those customers, and what it takes to perform well at that work.

We did not invest enough time in understanding our potential customers, and where they were already being served in a competitive landscape. We failed to be aware of external factors that would hurt us. Perhaps my biggest lessons were that:

- I came to realize how much I disliked cold calling, both for its low productivity and its high rejection rate.

- I came to realize how much I disliked trying to sell something people didn't know whether they wanted or needed.

- I enjoyed a 35 percent close rate in the training business, but that didn't translate like I thought it would in advertising. Knowing this weakness would become one of my critical guiding stars in future FranNet client work. Just because you're successful at something in one industry, while it should transfer well into another industry, it doesn't automatically happen. As part of your franchise ownership research, you need to understand the environment, market conditions, and most importantly, the work it takes as an owner to be successful in the business.

- I finally understood the risks and implications of taking on an unproven business model, in an unproven industry. This would become another one of my guiding stars in FranNet client work. The first five franchisees of any system are the alpha and beta tests of that business model; therefore, people *must* be prepared for much higher risk, because the nascent franchise model *will* evolve from the original, and not always the way one expects or hopes.

- Split focus has huge risks. Launching a new business while overseeing another (FranNet) takes a lot of time and energy, and it competes with family time. I underestimated the time it took to run both businesses simultaneously. I was very fortunate to have hired and trained a very competent associate to conduct all of the day-to-day client engagement work and partner relationship management at FranNet.

The failure of our mobile advertising business, and the lessons learned, would become new cornerstones to the coaching I've been providing to my FranNet clients since 2009.

Since 2017, I've been solely focused on my FranNet business. I continue to love the client work and enjoy a great lifestyle. This enabled me to adapt well when the COVID-19 pandemic hit. Every business owner had to pivot and find new ways to find new customers, and then find new ways to fulfill their services virtually. My FranNet business was no different. Fortunately, I've always done some client work from my home office. Instead of meeting clients face-to-face in my physical office suite, we just switched completely to digital meetings.

If you are a business owner, your awareness, resilience, and openness to new ways of thinking and doing were likely key factors in your survival. But it could be that many new ways of doing things will become sticky. As you will discover, for some franchisors "innovation" is not an easy word to hear from their franchisees. For others, building a learning culture is job one.

In chapter 2, I will introduce Driver No. 1: Grow a Next-Level Mindset. Franchisees illustrate how they are able to unlock potential and build a sustainable business with the right mindset. But before you move on to chapter 2, please complete the Growth Plan Exercise and the Personal Readiness Survey in the following pages.

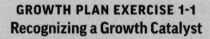

GROWTH PLAN EXERCISE 1-1
Recognizing a Growth Catalyst

A growth catalyst is a consequence of becoming aware that your current situation is no longer tenable, and where the pain of doing nothing is greater than the pain and sacrifice of making a significant change in your life or career. You will recall that when I was denied a raise at the bank, I realized at that moment corporate employment was no longer where I belonged. It was time for me to leave. In 1991 I had my second dance with experiencing a growth catalyst, where the difficulties of staying in the family business I was part of exceeded the difficulties of changing careers into the unknown. There have been several more throughout my entrepreneurial career, each driving me on to my next learning plateau.

What are your past growth catalysts that led you to buying your franchise? How much of that original motivating force is still present today? What new growth catalysts might be building now that you need to pay attention to? Take a few minutes to reflect on these questions and, while doing so, also reflect on how much you are giving to your business. Do you have time and energy to devote to your personal well-being and your family, or is there little time and energy left over for your family? Perhaps the seeds of your own growth catalyst can be found in your answers to these questions.

- What work are you doing that isn't fulfilling, or perhaps even demotivating to do?
- Conversely, what work is fulfilling and financially rewarding, and which you want to do more of?
- Do you have an income shortfall that you must get past, now?
- What can "give" in your business, so that you can make more time for your family and for yourself?
- Might you need to hire someone to reduce your personal work load?
- Might you need to talk through things with your spouse, and redefine expectations? Even if only for the short term while you make some changes?

Be sure to download the accompanying Growth Plan Workbook from theunstoppablefranchisee.com, which contains all of the surveys and exercises for you to complete; it also serves as your journal as you progress through the book. And keep your journal handy, because you'll hear from numerous top-performing franchisees on how they dealt with pain points and grew their business to the next level.

SURVEY 1-1:

Personal Readiness Survey for Starting or "Restarting" Your Own Business

Instructions: Whether you're seriously thinking about buying a franchise, or you already own one but the business is not delivering the outcomes you want, this exercise will help clarify elements that you need to take into consideration.

Underline the number that indicates your current level of activity, and highlight the number that indicates a reasonable goal for next-level growth.

	Almost Never	About 25% of the time	About 50% of the time	About 75% of the time	Almost Always
1. I stay focused on my original "why" or the purpose for starting my business.	1	2	3	4	5
2. I think about the personal energy I'll need to take something in my business to the next level.	1	2	3	4	5
3. I think about the effect taking something in my business to the next level will have on my family and work/life balance.	1	2	3	4	5
4. I think about the ways in which my skills can apply to taking my business to the next level.	1	2	3	4	5

	Almost Never	About 25% of the time	About 50% of the time	About 75% of the time	Almost Always
5. I think about the ways in which my accumulated experience and hard skills (e.g., technical) can apply to taking something in my business to the next level.	1	2	3	4	5
6. I think about the ways in which my soft skills (e.g., emotional intelligence) can apply to taking something in my business to the next level.	1	2	3	4	5
7. I think about the financial costs of taking something in my business to the next level.	1	2	3	4	5
8. I think about to what degree I'd need to manage additional risk and where my limitations are should I take something in my business to the next level.	1	2	3	4	5
9. I think about how taking something in my business to the next level might impact my income for a time, and if I have to make additional financial investment to do so.	1	2	3	4	5
10. I think about my personality and to what degree I can lead and support my team should I take something in my business to the next level.	1	2	3	4	5
11. I think about to what degree I can address more complex problems associated with taking something in my business to the next level.	1	2	3	4	5
12. I think about to what degree I am an effective collaborator.	1	2	3	4	5

	Almost Never	About 25% of the time	About 50% of the time	About 75% of the time	Almost Always
13. I think about to what degree I have the support of my family to take something in my business to the next level.	1	2	3	4	5
14. I think about how I'd be affected by and deal with the additional stress of taking something in my business to the next level.	1	2	3	4	5
15. I think about the right reasons for taking something in my business to the next level.	1	2	3	4	5

Out of the fifteen survey questions, list the five most urgent items that you believe you need to attend to. If you have a mentor or adviser, ask for their assessment and advice.

My most urgent items are:

1. _____

2. _____

3. _____

4. _____

5. _____

CHAPTER 2

DRIVER NO. 1
Grow a Next-Level Mindset

I'VE ALWAYS LOVED watching surfing competitions, especially big wave surfing like Jaws or the Pipeline in Hawaii or the Nazaré Tow Challenge in Portugal. Maybe it's the fascination with how these crazy people harness the massive energy of the monster waves, riding down the face of the wave balancing on a knife-edge piece of polystyrene foam wrapped in fiberglass. Maybe it's the thrill of the ride and the kudos in the surfing community, and the big-money sponsorships that come with success. These athletes risk everything to get out there and ride those big waves every chance they get, despite the fact that with one wrong move, the wave will deliver a crushing force that can, and does, kill. Every great surfer has had their share of dancing with the nasty side of this formidable force.

These surfers don't just start out by going out and trying to surf these huge waves. They've had years and years of practice. They started by surfing small waves, and progressively worked their way up. They have been trained by coaches and have, among many other things, learned how to read water and wave sets so they can pick out the best waves to surf. They have shared their knowledge and experience with their fellow surfers in that tight community. And yes, they have had plenty of wipeouts along the way, so they've also learned how to react to the turbulence underwater and get back to the surface so they can get on top of another awesome wave.

There are tons of good surfers out there; the greatest surfers dedicate themselves to becoming absolute masters of their craft by continually learning, by constantly and incrementally improving over time. They live and breathe a next-level mindset because their very lives depend upon doing so. And they get a shot at earning sponsors' big prize money for doing so.

Why am I drawing a picture about surfing? Because surfing is a metaphor for franchise ownership. The ocean is the marketplace, opportunities and challenges are the waves, and the business itself is the surfboard that the owner rides. The big-money and big-name sponsors are akin to franchisors. They have talent scouts, recruit promising talent, and provide support like coaching, mentoring, safety crews, and transportation. As the surfer develops talent, they drive more personal success and more prize income, and in turn the sponsors drive more brand value. The surfer is not left alone to figure things out and face the risks on their own; they have an entire team with a ton of expertise to help them compress their learning curve while accelerating the timeline to optimum performance and substantial financial success.

Good franchisors look and act a lot like the big-name sponsors. They are constantly seeking ways to increase brand value, so they have talent scouts to recruit promising new franchisees (franchise development executives—you've probably worked with one if you've already bought your franchise); they leverage the tremendous intellectual equity and collective brain trust of the entire franchise system to provide a vast amount of support, training, coaching, etc., which enables their franchisees to compress their learning curve while accelerating the timeline to higher optimum performance and financial success. Like the surfers supported by sponsors, franchisees are not left alone to figure things out and face the risks on their own because they too have an entire team with a ton of expertise.

There are two glaring differences (inconsistencies) in this metaphor, however:

· Surfing ocean waves is limited by the size of the waves available, whereas there is no limit to the size of market waves. The better the franchisee develops their next-level skills, the bigger the waves they can surf.

· Professional surfers get paid by the sponsors and earn prize money—the average income of a professional surfer is $250,000 to $400,000,[3] while the upper crust, the top ten male surfers of 2021, earned between $750,000 and $2.2 million.[4] Top-performing franchisees do not get paid by their franchisors; instead, they drive their own wealth by running successful businesses. And substantial financial success is not limited to the "top 10." Many top franchisees I've spoken with over the years consistently earn mid-six-figure to mid-seven-figure annual profits in their businesses.

Business owners are that small percentage of our society who are attracted to the thrill that comes with riding market waves. In North America, entrepreneurs make up roughly 10 percent of the total adult population and much of the other 90 percent thinks that entrepreneurs are crazy while at the same time looking at them with envy, thinking, "I wish I could do that. I wish I could have that level of control, independence and success." Roughly 10 percent of this entrepreneurial group is comprised of franchisees who have opted for the better likelihood of success that comes with franchising as opposed to starting a business from scratch. People who buy franchises typically want to accelerate learning how to ride the market waves by leveraging the knowledge and experience of the franchisor and existing franchisees who have gone before them.

The new franchisee learns how to surf the waves of the market by starting on small waves of opportunity and challenge, and then works their way up as they build their skills and confidence. Through trial and error, they learn to read the wave sets of the market and eventually can see which waves are surf-able and which ones to let pass them by. Franchisees with positive mindsets embrace getting out and surfing every day because they know that despite experiencing some wipeouts, bumps and bruises along the way, they're going to continually learn and get better at running their businesses. They catch bigger and bigger waves over time.

Franchisees with negative mindsets will go through the same learning journey, but will progress more slowly, will be less confident on their "board." Part of the reason is that they look for waves that can hurt them before seeing waves that can be surfed, and in so doing, miss riding some really good waves.

Next-Level Mindset—The Foundation of Success

Let's glean from this metaphor the importance of mindset. This is one of the most important factors to achieving super-performance; it is a core part of the foundation that all success is built upon.

As Greg Nathan, founder of the Franchise Relationships Institute, says, "It's this curiosity to learn from other people and [having the] humility to keep growing and striving to improve. Some people might call it a growth mindset these days, and that's this: 'I'm here to improve, improve, improve. I'm not here to prove how great I am.'"

NOT HERE TO PROVE HOW GREAT I AM

WHAT IS MINDSET?

Our mindset is the lens that we see, hear, feel, and experience our world through. It shapes our thoughts, opinions, and beliefs, and in so doing, predetermines our approach to the opportunities and challenges we face every day, in all areas of our lives. And it functions at the subconscious level, so most of the time we're not even aware of it shaping our thoughts, decisions and actions. Our mindset rarely surfaces to our conscious mind when facing an opportunity or challenge, which is why it's so important to look at in this chapter.

Carol Dweck, noted author and Stanford professor, identifies two major mindsets—fixed and growth.[5] In the years since her work was initially published, the subject of mindset has been broadly expanded upon, but what is consistent in most writings on this subject is that there is a direct correlation between what your mindset is and what your outcomes are. Let's explore why this matters, and how you can leverage it to substantially accelerate your business and personal development.

What is your initial response to a new opportunity or challenge? Is it oppositional, along the lines of "I can't do it" or "I'm just not good at this" or "Why does this keep happening to me?" Or is it encouraging, along the lines of "I can get through this," "I've dealt with things like this before," or "I'm learning how to get better at this"?

People with a fixed mindset believe their traits and abilities are fixed and can't be changed. Some fixed-mindset people also believe that talent and intelligence lead to their success, and not effort. On the flipside, people with a growth mindset believe that their talents and abilities can be developed over time through focused effort and determination. They believe that anyone can increase their intelligence and build their skills if they continue to work at it.[6]

In her article "Growth Mindset, Revisited," Dweck clarifies the concept of mindset: "Let's acknowledge that (1) we're all a mixture of fixed and growth mindsets, (2) we will probably always be, and (3) if we want to move closer to a growth mindset in our thoughts and practices, we need to stay in touch with our fixed-mindset thoughts and deeds."[7]

The definition that I feel captures mindset the best is from Mindsets.com: "Mind-sets are those collection[s] of beliefs and thoughts that make up the mental attitude, inclination, habit or disposition that predetermines a person's interpretations and responses to events, circumstances and situations."[8] However small or large a task or decision, we approach it with a sense of what the possible outcomes could be and whether or not we will be successful. You can see how strongly mindset affects our behaviors and actions.

....

"If you think you can do a thing or think you can't do a thing, you're right." HENRY FORD

....

The great news is that mindsets are not static or constant. Once we become aware of our current mindset, we can make incremental adjustments and refine it so that it serves us better over time. In other words, we can make a conscious choice to cultivate a different mindset—we evolve it.

GROWTH PLAN EXERCISE 2-1
Which way do you see your environment?

Take a few minutes to reflect on your current mindset. Are you generally more a "glass half-full" or a "glass half-empty" person? Are you more likely to approach change and risk by looking for obstacles first and thoroughly analyzing the situation before seeing the positive outcome possibilities? Or are you more likely to look for the positive outcomes first, and then look for obstacles?

Author Simon Sinek has said, "There are two ways to see the world. Some people see the things they want. Some people see the thing that prevents them from getting what they want."[9]

When Les Stroud, one of the world's leading survival experts, says, "There's nothing that can beat you like your own mind,"[10] I bet you he's referring to Sinek's second group.

Which of Sinek's two camps do you fall into?

Regardless of what your current mindset is, it's good to become aware of this now, so that you can anchor back to it as you use the drivers of this book to build your growth journey. Know that any progressive or positive shifts you make to your mindset, however small, will make substantial and lasting improvements to your levels of personal and business success.

Conversely, any negative or unfavorable shifts you allow to happen in your mindset will cause substantial and lasting erosion of your personal and business success.

Why is this? Because humans crave feedback in all that we do, and our future actions are based on how we perceive our current experiences and results. We are creatures of feedback loops; our mindset sets the frame in which we accept and process our feedback.

CREATURES OF FEEDBACK LOOPS

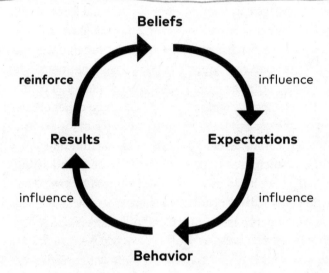

The self-fulfilling prophecy feedback loop (a concept introduced by American sociologist Robert K. Merton in 1948[11]) shows how our beliefs influence our expectations; how our expectations influence behavior and actions; how our actions influence results; and how our results reinforce and reconfirm our beliefs. This is a classic example of a feedback loop. The more that we repeat the cycle without changing any of its components, the more we reinforce each and make the pattern more permanent—in other words, a habit, hence the name "self-fulfilling prophecy."

....

"We first make our habits and then our habits make us." JOHN DRYDEN

"Attitudes are nothing more than habits of thought." JOHN C. MAXWELL

....

But remember, a mindset is not static or permanent. There are ways to step out of a feedback loop.

BREAKING THE PATTERN

Short-term change can happen when an external force is applied to three of the four components—Expectations, Behavior, and Results. Once that external force is removed, it is our human nature to revert to the original pattern. More durable change happens when the external force is applied to Beliefs, because when you change your beliefs, that change transmits through all of the other elements.

The COVID-19 pandemic is a great example of an external force. Why did some franchisees flourish as the pandemic progressed, while other franchisees within the exact same brand struggled or even failed? This phenomenon was not limited to any one sector. I saw examples of it in commercial cleaning, in the sign industry, in fast food/quick-serve restaurants, and in business coaching, just to name a few.

Education and training too are examples of external forces. As you learn new skills, the expectation that you can perform new tasks increases, which triggers more focus and concentration as you do the new work, which then yields better results. Those better results give you an extra boost of confidence and that increases your belief in yourself that you can do better.

This is the essence of the next-level mindset that you'll see time and time again throughout this book.

Internal forces also apply here—getting in touch with your *why* is an example. When you become clearer on your whys for achieving a goal, it's human nature to then become more assertive in seeking the knowledge, people, money, and time needed to achieve the goal, which increases your expectations, and so on.

One's mindset does not have to be fixed; it is something that is malleable, and that can be strengthened (or weakened) over time. Top-performing franchisees are acutely aware of their mindset and can read the forces that influence it. Their curiosity and desire to learn nurtures it consistently.

It's not just about having a positive mindset. While that is definitely part of it, it's how you apply that mindset to your own growth path; it's how you "surf" the waves of opportunity and challenges that come your way.

Next-Level Mindset Defined

Of all the material I researched on mindset, the most applicable is from Enrique Rubio, the founder of Hacking HR, which he dubs the Evolving Mindset: "The Evolving Mindset sets the stage for a new kind of thinking and learning process in which all of us have the absolute potential to achieve the kind of success we seek. The Evolving Mindset is a thinking process; it revolves around several essential premises: a quest for knowledge, inner curiosity, open-mindedness for failure and humility for success, and Cyclic Learning."[12]

My next-level mindset concept builds on Rubio's model. In addition to a thinking and learning process, it is an action and behavior process that is being clearly demonstrated by every top-performing franchisee I've encountered. But it doesn't happen immediately. Top performers weren't always top performers. Most started at the same baseline as every other new franchisee and had to go through the same training to learn the business systems and processes. The way they progressed is what we'll examine here so that you can begin mirroring what helped create their success.

The next-level mindset is one that opens our awareness of possibilities, despite limitations. It is the mindset of the purposeful, of the calculated risk-taker, of the confident. It is one of embracing setbacks, seeking both to overcome and to capture the lesson within the setback while doing so. It is one of embracing opportunity, seeking both to maximize the outcome and to capture the opportunity's lesson too, for without seeking the lessons, we risk becoming stagnant.

For you as a franchisee, it means finding ways to remain true to the brand and to the playbook, while finding ways to adapt when needed to capitalize upon opportunity or overcome challenge. It is the mindset that enables you to recognize opportunities and challenges and to focus the resources you have on the most impactful ones.

I chose the term "next-level mindset" intentionally, because this is about moving from where you currently are to where you want to get to—in results, in work/life integration and balance, etc. I'm talking about the very nature of constantly evolving to your next level.

Evolution occurs slowly—one step at a time, one focus area at a time, one attempt at a time, one change at a time, one increase in awareness at a time—until new thought and behavior patterns displace the old patterns. It is continuing to do what you know works, while experimenting around the edges so that you can get to your next level.

....

"Progress is impossible without change, and those who cannot change their minds cannot change anything." GEORGE BERNARD SHAW

....

The Top-Performer Mindset on Growth

Growth is a natural and necessary component of any successful business, and of any successful entrepreneur and business leader. All meaningful growth takes focused effort, pain and sacrifice, and for the vast majority of us, this is how we've accumulated our knowledge throughout our entire lives in order to do things differently. We learn from experimenting around the edges; we learn from the mistakes and successes that result. We also learn by consistently applying the next-level mindset.

Growth in business also must be rooted and anchored in something—in values, in vision, in purpose. These anchors will be different for each owner, and when fully developed create a contagious energy and focus that employees and customers gravitate to. They sense the commitment to excellence and believe they have a part in it.

ANGELA BROWN: THE NEXT-LEVEL MINDSET IN ACTION

Angela Brown is a top franchisee of Blo Blow Dry Bar. The franchise opened its first store in 2007 and now has more than one hundred locations in the US and Canada. Let's examine Angela's next-level mindset through the pillars of the feedback loop:

- *Have a clear vision and a big goal.* (Beliefs): Angela says, "A lot of it has to do with having a clear vision on where you're trying to get to. You have to have a vision that's audacious, something that pushes the envelope. If it doesn't scare you, it's not big enough."

- *Have commitment and focus.* (Expectations): "I call it my daily discipline, things that I do every single day, that I know, over time, will get me there. I have to force my brain to do the small things, and I'm not really wired to think like that. I'm a big picture thinker, so for me to drill it down to daily disciplines, I need to trust in the process. I teach my managers the same mindset."

- *Align leadership and vision among the team.* (Behavior): "As a leader, it's my responsibility to have the vision as to where I want the company to go and to grow. Then, when I find people that I think may be a fit for the team, I need to find out where their vision lies. We all lead our own lives, and so I want to know what their vision is. Then we try to find some alignment. It becomes my responsibility as the leader to make sure that they're able to actualize their individual goals and their vision for where they want to go with the company's goals."

- *Servant leadership is what this is all about.* (Behavior): "Servant leadership sings to my heart. That's what this is all about. We serve others. That's the bottom line." (See chapter 5 for more on servant leadership.)

- *Articulate what you value.* (Expectations): "I think it's important to have clarity on what you value at the core—what is your motivator, what's going to get your engine fired up... I can set goals as big as the moon and it doesn't scare me, because at the end of the day I'm going to live and die by my values and my convictions."

It's plain to see that Angela has created her formula for next-level thinking and growth based on her core values. They give her confidence and conviction, and that kind of attitude drives like-minded thinking among her teams and has delivered great results for her and her franchisor.

SAROSH NAYAR: THE NEXT-LEVEL MINDSET IN ACTION

Sarosh Nayar is a top-performing franchisee of FASTSIGNS. Of the seven hundred FASTSIGNS in the world, Sarosh's franchise is the third-best performer. Let's examine his next-level mindset.

- *The attitude you bring to your business.* (Beliefs): He says, "I think attitude is everything. When employees come in every day, they set the tone with their attitude. And as leader, you've got to set the right attitude—you set the direction for your company. I think one long face can really pull the team down, especially when times are tough. When I'm building a team, the right attitude is something I'm focused on."

- *Think big.* (Expectations): "We want to be one of the top FAST-SIGNS in the world. With seven hundred FASTSIGNS, we're No. 3 in the world. And we still want to grow."

- *Invest in your business.* (Behavior): "Invest in the right technology and machinery and tools that can make you more efficient and grow your business, and that can allow you to introduce new products and services to your customers profitably. So right up front, that was the mindset going into the business—I will forgo short-term profits for a longer-term investment."

- *Be innovative.* (Behavior): "We have the ability to influence customers based on our thinking and coming to them with innovative ideas, innovative new materials, and keeping up to date with what's going on in the industry in terms of products and services. This helps you present a solution to the customer that perhaps they were not necessarily thinking of."

- *Delight your customers.* (Behavior): "You must delight your customers. Part of it is being innovative, the ability to delight your customers at every touch point. It starts with the attitude, how you pick up the phone and how you talk to customers, and the delivery of the products on time, meeting and exceeding all of the customer's requirements. And that leads to having long-term customers and repeat business."

Sarosh operates a winning franchise and his behaviors and expectations directly lead to the results he's experiencing—because that's what he expects and it shows in how he chooses to act.

IN CHAPTER 3, we will expand on the link between mindset and awareness, with practical examples of its application. Before you leave this chapter, please complete the Growth Plan Exercise and the survey.

GROWTH PLAN EXERCISE 2-2: Assess Your Core Values

Reflect on the following excerpt from the interview with Angela Brown. How would you express the point Angela is making?

> I think it's important to have clarity on what you value at the core, what is your motivator, what's going to get your engine fired up, so that's the core. Where the tough part comes in, is once you do that part, you have to write a narrative as to why you value those things. That's where you get rooted to your conviction and to your values. The more you can explain the reason why you value those things, the more convicted and the more solid you'll be in your belief around those, that's where courage and confidence come from.

- What are your core values?
- Why do you hold these values?
- How do these values impact your business decisions?
- Where might there be incongruity that needs to be assessed?

SURVEY 2-1:

How Well Does Your Mindset Prepare You to Achieve Operational Excellence?

On a scale of 1 (not at all prepared) to 10 (fully prepared)	Minimally 1-4	Moderately 5-7	Highly 8-10
1. I am motivated to grow my business to the next level.			
2. I am confident that there is clear alignment between my personal values and the business.			
3. I am confident that I have the right people on my team to grow the business.			
4. I am confident that my business fundamentals are sound.			
5. I am confident that my business cannot be disrupted.			
6. I am confident that I have a firm understanding of the business's finances.			
7. I am confident that I understand the barriers to next-level growth I may face.			
8. I am confident that I have enough capital to grow my business to the next level.			
9. I am confident that I can grow my existing customer base.			
10. I am confident that I can grow my people and inspire them to do more.			

SURVEY RESULTS: This survey builds on your answers from the survey in chapter 1. It is designed to help you develop greater personal insight into running your business, which includes the initiative and drive to continuously improve the business. By noting potential weaknesses, you will be able to apply more focus to those topics in this book and then purposefully close the gaps.

Driver No. 1 Takeaways

List your top three takeaways from this chapter:

1. _____

2. _____

3. _____

DRIVER NO. 2
Grow Your Awareness

MICHAEL GILPIN, a franchisee with FASTSIGNS, is a great example of having a continuous improvement mindset. His actions are centered on "doing everything you can to be better tomorrow than you were today, and better today than you were yesterday." In order to do this, he and his FASTSIGNS group like to keep things in perspective with a quote from Rory Vaden in *Take the Stairs*: "Success is not owned. Success is rented. And the rent is due every day."[13]

How are awareness and success related? For Michael, awareness is linked to customer experience—it is the ability to read a situation and anticipate what outcomes are likely, whether it is with a customer, vendor, or team member. This ability to anticipate also creates a self-awareness that can help franchisees make critical decisions in the face of difficult circumstances.

As Michael says, "Anticipation is preparing you to be aware. Knowing that in a certain situation we could be over here. 'Am I ready to be over here?' Instead of, in that certain situation, all of a sudden we're over here, and the thinking is: 'How in the heck did I get here?'" The difference to Michael is one in which awareness is working on multiple levels—being aware of the larger-scale situation *and* your own ability to act in relation to it. Without this multi-level awareness, your actions are no longer calculated but reactive, and that can be a dangerous place.

The most successful franchisees and business owners have honed their awareness to a level that enables them to achieve admirable levels of success. Every one of the TPFs I interviewed agreed that awareness is a critical factor in their success; some, like Clara Osterhage, Great Clips's No. 1 franchisee with over eighty salons, even described it as their sixth sense. As you progress through this chapter, you'll hear from numerous franchisees as to how awareness is critical to their next-level growth and how you can apply their insights and lessons.

A Neural Network for Your Business

We are genetically designed to be aware—of pain, pleasure, opportunity, or threat. We seek safety, pleasure, and comfort; we avoid pain and threat. The human body's highly complex neural network provides us with five senses so that we can constantly observe, take in, process, and respond/react to the environment around us. Our body's nervous system is loaded with nerve receptors, which fire when pain or pleasure is physically experienced:

- When we experience pain, our neural network's pain receptors fire in response to an injury or hurtful condition. The intensity of the signals from those nerve receptors is commensurate with the severity of the injury and bodily threat. The signals travel instantaneously from the injured part of our body to our brain. Awareness is instantaneous.

- Our body's pleasure sensors perform in the exact same manner as our pain sensors. The signals travel instantaneously from the positively activated part of our body to our brain.

We experience various forms of pain and pleasure, and at varying levels of intensity. Responding to our neural signals is often a reflex, but sometimes we must consciously process what those signals are telling us. Based on information at hand, we make decisions about how to respond. Think about putting your hand on a hot stove. The immediate response is to yank your hand away. Imagine that your pain sensors in your hand weren't firing and you leave your hand on the stove until you smell flesh burning.

What if it's possible to develop a similar neural network for your business? One that helps you become more aware of opportunities and threats, both internal and external? Without it, how will you know when you're having a "hand on hot stove" moment, and don't know that something critical is burning?

Canoe Trip Gone Wrong

I love the outdoors, the solitude and the peace that comes with being completely immersed in nature. I also love watching survival shows; one of my favorites is *Survivorman*, where Les Stroud goes off-grid on his own for a period of seven to ten days and teaches his viewers how to survive in potentially life-threatening situations.

Several years ago, while on a solo backcountry canoe trip, I fell down in the rapids while lining my canoe (I should have taken the portage) and smashed my knee against a rock. I couldn't immediately tell how severe the injury was, but one thing I knew was that I was in a great deal of pain. I eventually made it to shore and was able to take a moment to assess my situation. I asked myself, "Is this my *Survivorman* moment?" The pain was intense; I couldn't put any pressure on my knee. I had a forty-five-pound backpack and a slightly heavier canoe, there were three long portages ahead of me, and I was on a route where I was unlikely to encounter anyone. On top of that I was out of range for cell service. I began wondering if I would be able to get home, or even get out. I was incredibly lucky that day because it turned out to be only a severely bruised knee-cap; after a couple of hours the pain dissipated and I was able to continue, albeit more slowly. It was a watershed awareness moment for me; afterwards, I swore that I would never be so unprepared again, and I began studying bushcraft skills in earnest.

Of the hundreds of hours of bushcraft and survival shows and videos I've watched, one of the best and easiest-to-remember methodologies to use in a critical survival situation is Survivorman's Zones of Assessment™ model:[14]

- Zone 1: assessing what you have on your person
- Zone 2: assessing what's in your immediate surroundings, such as your car, bike, canoe, etc.
- Zone 3: assessing what might be accessible nearby (a short walk away)

I like to think of this level of awareness as "aware-sense," or becoming aware of and making sense of your immediate surroundings—surroundings that you weren't initially aware of but that upon closer inspection you can use should you find yourself in a critical, high-risk situation. This heightened aware-sense can enable you to survive and get out of danger.

You might be thinking, "Okay, Gary, but why is this important in business?"

Well, while running a business should rarely be about getting yourself out of a high-risk situation (though it may happen from time to time), it is about making informed decisions that enable you to thrive through any market conditions. Where Stroud's three-zone model is applicable in his environment, you'll see how with aware-sense at its core, my four-zone assessment model will help you create a neural network for your business. This model will provide a deeper perspective on your business and identify where to make changes to run it more effectively, and maybe even to levels you might have previously thought impossible. I base my model on this assertion: The quality of inbound information determines the quality of operational decisions and their direct outcomes.

DEVELOPING EXPONENTIAL AWARE-SENSE

Running a business is akin to flying a plane; pilots are trained to be fully aware of everything around them, including how the plane is operating. They operate in a multidimensional environment with numerous forces acting upon the plane that need to be managed, all the while maintaining control and reaching their destination. A pilot has a full instrumentation panel to assist them in their task, and with a quick glance a pilot can determine their altitude, speed, direction, and whether the plane is climbing, banking or descending. The attitude indicator is a critical instrument because it gives the pilot a clear picture of the aircraft's wing position relative to the earth's horizon. The plane's attitude determines its altitude. Remember this critical statement.

As a business owner, you are also operating in a multidimensional environment. Where an airplane pilot has to maintain flight by taking into account wind, air density, gravity, and engine output, you have to take into account complex forces like competition, labor and supply chain shortages, cash flow and technology/innovation to maintain your business. The more aware you are of how your business is "flying" amidst these market forces, the more quickly you can make mid-flight adjustments to ensure that you stay on your intended course—so you need an effective instrument panel. You likely already have one, but you might not be getting enough valid and critical information.

I hear of far too many franchisees who are stuck at their current levels of performance because they're afraid to invest money into achieving their next-level growth. I suggest that this is largely because their available business information is inadequate, and resulting awareness gaps prevent them from gaining additional business velocity. This contributes to insufficient confidence to proceed with investing further in their business; instead, they're just struggling to maintain their status quo.

Improving the quality and amount of information to help you run your business more efficiently may be far easier said than done; I can assure you, though, that doing so is an important early step in developing stronger aware-sense in your business. As your aware-sense develops, the pace at which you'll make purposeful and conscious decisions, and better decisions, to drive better results will increase. Franchisee Joel Winters says, "The ability to make decisions quickly without procrastinating is a really key thing, because then you know if you've succeeded or failed a lot more quickly. Then you can repeat that process and continue to make decisions."

It's not just about assessment, though. Once you've got better clarity on what's happening within your business, whether you're experiencing business pleasure or bleeding from business pain, you'll be able to rapidly identify where your focus of primary resources should shift to. You should also have greater confidence in the decisions that will need to be made when it comes to making investments into those shifts.

A big part of developing aware-sense is assessing performance and seeking the lessons from the experience, whether positive or negative.

How to Use the Aware-sense Four-Zone Model

If you've been piloting your business up until now without a full instrument panel, then presenting you with a model to run your business better might initially be overwhelming. Like the pilot, though, once you've got some decent flying time in with using your new instruments, you'll wonder how you ever managed without them.

The intent of each of these assessment zones is for you to assess your present position in relation to where you want or need to be. The four assessment zones in the aware-sense model are:

- Aware-sense Zone 1: Internal, Personal
- Aware-sense Zone 2: Internal, Business
- Aware-sense Zone 3: External, Local Market Opportunities and Forces
- Aware-sense Zone 4: External, National/Global Market Forces

Utilizing these assessments is not a one-time thing. Top-performing franchisees assess their position constantly. This should become an exercise you revisit frequently, especially when you're about to take on a new project or growth curve.

As you personalize each of your zones, you'll be building an integral part of your business's dashboard or instrument panel to measure what really matters for your specific business. While there are myriad things that can get measured, as you use this tool more frequently you will come to understand which ones need just an occasional glance and which need regular observation.

In completing the following exercises, which cover each aware-sense zone, know that there are no wrong answers; instead, recognize that this is your current starting aware-sense point as you get ready to enter your next-level growth phase. Be honest with your answers; this will help you identify where the biggest areas for improvement and personal growth lie.

AWARE-SENSE ZONE 1: INTERNAL, PERSONAL

The information derived from this zone is critical to the levels of success, health, happiness, and peace that we can achieve, so I'll go more deeply into this zone than the others. This is also the most personal zone—it's where we keep our most private thoughts and beliefs.

It's important to start with assessing what personal resources you have available to you. These resources are:

- Mental/Intellectual: This aspect includes things like your motivation level, core skills, composite of attitudes, and your mindset, which we explored in the last chapter.
- Physical: This aspect includes the time you make available for your business, your level of physical energy, and the personal finances that you're prepared to inject into the business.

Before we begin exploring this topic, let me share a deeply personal belief. In my teen years, my dad and I would have talks about all kinds of things. When we talked about my ambitions, hopes and dreams, this was the essence of his message to me, which I've carried with me throughout my life and career and which has been a key part of success I've achieved and failures I've rebounded from:

If something has been done before, then someone has already proven that a human being is physically capable of doing it, so that means it's physically possible for you to do as well. You just have to decide whether or not you want to do that something; if you do, then start doing it to the best of your abilities. Recognize, though, that on some days your "best" won't be as good as other days, so it's okay to fail. As long as you keep trying, and learning from your efforts, only you determine the limits that you will rise to.

GROWTH PLAN EXERCISE 3-1
List Mental/Intellectual Resources

Nobody is good at everything, but many franchisees and business owners get so caught up in the day-to-day work that they're stuck working *in* their business instead of *on* their business. In the following exercise, take your time to reflect on the questions and then provide your answers.

1. What types of work activity are you really good at? List those activities that would lift your business by giving them more time and attention.

2. What other work or personal activities are preventing you from investing more time doing these impactful activities?

3. What types of work activity are you not good at or would rather not do, but that currently consume too much of your time? Why are you doing these activities instead of delegating them or contracting them out?

4. Next-level mindset: As I stated in chapter 2, a growth mindset and awareness are closely linked. A next-level mindset enables you to decide what goals to pursue; awareness enables you to prioritize, and where to bring your time, money, people, and physical resources to bear—and where and when to reallocate when necessary. Growth is a natural and necessary component of any successful business, and meaningful growth takes focused effort, pain and sacrifice, and for most of us this is how we've accumulated our

knowledge throughout our entire lives in order to do things differently, to learn through successes, to learn through mistakes, and to consistently apply the next-level mindset. How would you describe how actively you pursue your goals and overcome your challenges? Do you avoid setting goals and confronting challenges?

5. The correlation between motivation, purpose, and attaining success was evidenced by nearly every one of the TPFs I interviewed. For example, many of the interviewees talked about how building a legacy for their family was an important motivator. Another motivator was the ability to look after their people and to serve others; and yet another was achieving success by growing the business. All of the TPFs had absolute clarity on their purpose for being in business and how their goals, which they monitor relentlessly, move their business forward. Describe your original motivation and goals, and then compare this to your current purpose for running your business.

6. Motivation levels: What got you excited about buying your business might not be enough to keep you excited now. Over time, as your business evolves and your motivators change, if you cannot find new reasons to stay motivated, then excitement, energy and focus wane. Too often this results in declining business performance and results. Describe your current level of motivation to run your business, and think about how you have maintained or increased your level of motivation. If the opposite is true, then describe why your level of motivation has declined.

SURVEY 3-1:
Attitudes and Behaviors Assessment

I believe that there's no such thing as an overall good or bad attitude; instead, we each have a series of attitudes that, combined, shape our logic and decision-making. These include our attitudes and behaviors around time management, the use of technology, caring for our health, and how we see ourselves as a leader, among others. Attitudes and behaviors are not fixed. Your current attitude towards a thing is your autopilot; it predetermines your course and likely outcome, until and unless you decide to take some type of action to alter your course. You can change an attitude or behavior; it takes focus, discipline and time, but it can and will happen. Remember, in flying, the plane's attitude determines its altitude; the same is true for you personally, and for your business.

Because Exponential Aware-sense Zone 1 begins with assessing your current attitude towards a number of critical components, use this survey to assess your personal attitudes and behaviors in these areas. Use the blank lines in the grid to add your own factors. After that, the flying metaphor continues with discussion of two instruments on your business panel.

On a scale of 1 (not a priority) to 10 (a top priority), what level of priority do you ascribe to the following?	Low 1–4	Medium 5–7	High 8–10
1. Maintaining good health, including diet and exercise.			
2. Maintaining high levels of mental and physical energy.			
3. Setting SMART personal and business goals. SMART is Specific, Measurable, Achievable, Realistic, and Time-bound.			
4. Time management.			
5. Maintaining focus and capably managing distractions.			
6. Overall commitment to the work required.			
7. Ability to execute a sound marketing strategy to attract prospective clients.			
8. Ability to sell by converting prospects into clients.			

On a scale of 1 (not a priority) to 10 (a top priority), what level of priority do you ascribe to the following?	Low 1–4	Medium 5–7	High 8–10
9. Executing on day-to-day operations management.			
10. Managing money, both on a personal and a business level.			
11. Adding to knowledge of new technologies and ease of use with current technology.			
12. Exhibiting a consistently high standard of leadership.			
13. Managing your risk tolerance and approach to risk.			
14. Maintaining clarity on your values and living them every day.			
15. Avoiding self-judgment and understanding that you are not going to solve every problem every day.			
16.			
17.			

SURVEY RESULTS: Keep this survey handy. These topics are addressed throughout the book, and you will be given tips to make necessary changes to reprioritize critical aspects of running your business.

INSTRUMENT 1: ATTITUDE INDICATOR

Do you have an abundance mentality or a scarcity mentality? Top-performing franchisees do not bow to the external force of others' judgment or beat themselves up over things not yet achieved or realized; they have a next-level mindset and are highly internally motivated and focused on constant growth—on something. That "something" is dictated by how they set, plan, and achieve and surpass their objectives, both professionally and personally. It is not a point in time; rather, it is an ongoing journey. And along the way, they experience fear, doubt and uncertainty; they also experience excitement and believe they can achieve, so they get on with doing what's necessary. Not falling victim to negative thoughts is one sign of an abundance mentality. It is a mentality that will never succumb to weaknesses or excuses. It is a mentality rooted in potential.

Let's also consider what a scarcity mindset looks like. One of my clients bought a business in late 2020 and was supposed to open in January 2021. He couldn't open until May, though, due to a number of factors, some COVID-related, some through human error. This client was always anticipating the negative, so I suggested he read a book on manifesting titled *The Secret* by Rhonda Byrne. He told me he didn't have time to read it.

Several weeks later, challenges continued to be encountered, and this client said something to me that I'll never forget, because it illustrated profoundly how much our mindset can work against us. He said, "If it weren't for bad luck, I wouldn't have any luck at all." He was certainly looking at the downside of every situation instead of seeing the possibilities. The good news is that he finally hit positive cash flow in September 2021, so somewhere along the way he was able to make some adjustments.

Abundance: To what degree do you possess an abundance mentality? Where do you land on the Abundance Scale?

ABUNDANCE SCALE

1 ———————Scarcity ————— 50 | 51 ——————Abundance ————— 100

Optimism: Do you believe things are possible and likely, and therefore achievable for you, or are you more doubtful? Where are you on the Optimism Scale?

OPTIMISM SCALE

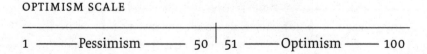

1 ———————Pessimism ————— 50 | 51 ——————Optimism ————— 100

INSTRUMENT 2: MOTIVATION INDICATOR: The Performance
Journey Bell Curve

....

**"All progress takes place outside the
comfort zone." MICHAEL JOHN BOBAK**

....

Let's look at a performance journey—specifically the aspect of
engagement and what happens when engagement decreases. The
door at the bottom left in the graph below represents when someone comes into a new organization; the line represents how they
progress over time through their work journey within the company.
This holds as true for any new franchisee as it does for any employee.

This curving line, called the engagement curve, represents a
person's performance journey through four quadrants over time,
a journey that can lead to suboptimal performance if detrimental
behaviors are left unchecked.

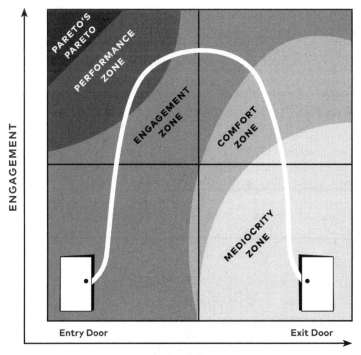

QUADRANT 1: High Engagement, Low Skills. When someone is presented with a new opportunity (for example, starting a new job or launching a new business), they are in the Engagement Zone. They are highly motivated to do well, but they and their franchise support coach (or manager if not self-employed) know they need to grow some specific skills through training and experience. Their results remain comparatively low while they focus on building their skills, knowledge and relationships. As they gain skills, experience and ability, they increase their performance levels and get ready to progress to the next quadrant. Depending on the complexity of the role, people will remain in Quadrant 1 from three to eighteen months, with six to nine months being a more typical time frame. This is likely familiar to you as you recall your early days in a new business or job.

QUADRANT 2: Highest Engagement, Highest Skills. Once someone has developed enough of the required skills, knowledge and relationships in Quadrant 1, they proceed to Quadrant 2, where they become more productive and retain a mostly positive mindset. They are still in the Engagement Zone, albeit performing at higher levels because of increased skills. (Some people will feel overwhelmed and must find the internal wherewithal to keep going.) Motivated to continue to build their skills, while in this quadrant people are highly focused on next-level growth and the highest return on their effort and activities. (Note: It is not always about money; for many people, quality of lifestyle is even more important.)

People in Quadrant 2 who possess the highest levels of motivation, focus, and drive to continually improve also have higher levels of optimism than most. They are the top 20 percent who evolve from the Engagement Zone to the Performance Zone.

People in this quadrant live by principles of self-accountability and self-responsibility.

The best of the best evolve to "Pareto's Pareto"—the 80/20 of the 80/20, or the top 4 percent. These people are truly living and breathing every aspect of the next-level mindset.

Graham Cooke, vice president of new restaurant expansion for A&W, characterizes the top 4 percent of performers this way:

> I think the best franchisees, that 4 percent, are the ones that can actually see beyond their own business, sit on the council with their fellow franchisees, and help the company make quality, superior national decisions that, in some cases, might even adversely affect their own business. Your best franchisees will understand that, while it may affect their own business, such a decision is the right thing to do for the system. So, they almost become a second tier of corporate thinkers about the success of the total enterprise.

QUADRANT 3: High Skills, Moderate Engagement. When people find themselves in this quadrant, they are still highly motivated and highly engaged, but they may be starting to stagnate. This could be from a lack of new challenges (boredom), lack of available upward mobility, or myriad other factors. This is the very essence of a comfort zone, and where an awareness of being unhappy creeps in. If the individual does not seek or receive coaching or mentoring and this condition is left to fester, the individual will decline into Quadrant 4, because downward momentum builds and increases in energy, which depletes the energy needed for focusing on the tasks at hand. The result is that performance naturally declines. Mary Thompson, the COO of Neighborly, suggests this condition is dangerous because the franchisee may be thinking they don't need you (the franchisor) and as a result are likely not following the system.

Top performers are aware of the danger of becoming complacent or too comfortable, and seize the prospect of entering the comfort zone as an opportunity to refocus on next-level growth. In essence, they loop back to the engagement zone of Quadrants 1 and 2, just at a higher level on their own Growth Helix, and thus maintain high motivation from experiencing new challenges, learning new skills, and gaining more ability to achieve even higher performance levels.

When things get too routine or too familiar, it's natural for the franchisee to look for other activities to keep them busy or intellectually engaged... and often that ends up being things that are not healthy for the business. Sean Hassan, one of Jan-Pro Franchise Development's top regional developers, shares this perspective:

> Plan for boredom. If you're doing things right, you'll get bored, right? When you let go of things, you trust other people to do things and your business is running autonomously... because everyone's doing everything. So you have to plan for that. Because if you don't plan for it, it's going to destroy you [by shifting focus to nonproductive work]. And the cool thing about boredom... that's when you can become the most creative. So I've come up with some great ideas... and so many of those crazy daily ideas are now day-to-day practices of my staff.

Neighborly developed an internal training program that is based in *Shoshin*. Mary explains: "It's the practice of the beginner's mind. When you think you know everything, come back and look at it from the beginner's mind. So they follow the system and you bring them back to the system time and again." It's easy to extrapolate that Sean Hassan practices *Shoshin* to avoid sliding into a less productive comfort zone.

QUADRANT 4: Waning Skills, Low/No Engagement. The lowest performers in an organization, who are usually some of the unhappiest people, are in this quadrant. They are also dangerous, because the prevalent attitude among those in the Mediocrity Zone can erode the mindset and behaviors of productive franchisees. They broadcast and foster the "Ain't it awful!" syndrome and are quick to pick at threads of unhappiness and point out what's wrong in others' lives. It's easier for them to pull other people down into their misery than it is to make the efforts and sacrifices needed to improve their current condition. They live in a world of blame and denial, rarely accepting responsibility for their own lack of performance.

If you have employees like these in your franchise, this is a critical problem that requires immediate attention. Explore every possible way to motivate and move them back to the Engagement Zone. If you can't, then you will want to explore exiting them from your franchise.

GROWTH PLAN EXERCISE 3-2
Performance Journey Locator

Top performers aspire to the top 4 percent of the performance journey and motivate their people to join them. Where are you in your own performance journey? If you're not in Quadrant 2, what needs to change to get there (or back there)?

- If you're in Quadrant 1, what steps can you take to increase engagement in the business even further? For example, are you experiencing issues with time management, staff retention, cash flow, etc. that are affecting your focus on growing the business?

- If you're in Quadrant 2, what have you mastered and can continue to excel at? What still needs work? What can you delegate that yields lower results than your best-talent areas?

- If you're in Quadrant 3, the same questions apply as Quadrant 2, plus which action steps you or your field coach have identified that, with hard work and dedication, can move you back onto the engagement curve, although at the next level up on your personal Growth Helix. For example, where can you locate your key employees on their performance journey within your business? What about the rest of your employees? Which next-level growth areas have you already identified that have the most potential for getting you back into Quadrant 1, and from there recharging so that you can progress to Quadrant 2?

- If you have employees who are in Quadrant 4, they're in crisis, and thus you are as well. Can you and they work together to find a path back to Quadrant 2, or do you need to make tougher decisions?

- For any franchisee that identifies with being in Quadrant 4, it probably feels like you're always fighting fires. You have some critical decisions to make. Can you find your *Shoshin*, your beginner's mind, and work with your franchisor and your team to find a path back to Quadrant 2? A starting point might be to reconnect to why you originally opened your business. Do you want to get back on track—really want to? Are you still driven enough? Do you even want to try? How open are you to extra coaching support from your franchisor? From other franchisees as potential mentors? How prepared are you to be vulnerable and admit you've made mistakes that need correcting?

Use the Performance Journey Locator tool to identify and prioritize additional next-level growth areas. This can also be a great tool for communicating with your franchisor's support team to help you improve, or for 1-on-1 coaching with your staff, getting them to rate themselves and answer the same questions. You can then compare notes and come up with a growth plan for each key employee.

How you answer these questions will help determine your immediate path. If you still have some spirit and drive left, and you want to recover, you'll be able to start exploring resources available. If the answer is no, you don't want to make any changes, then the best course of action might be to work with your franchisor to explore exiting your business as amicably as possible.

As Brad Rush, a regional developer at Jan-Pro, says about self-awareness: "It's a matter of people being honest with themselves and asking, 'Am I really willing to put in the time and effort?' Because it's not just going to magically come to fruition without some really disciplined, hard, consistent work."

BEHAVIORAL DATA
(PERSONALITY ASSESSMENT) INSTRUMENTS

Gaining awareness about the traits and abilities that drive successful performance in actionable terms offers advantages to realizing stronger performance in any role in a franchise. Chuck Russell, one of the world's leading authorities on the business applications of behavioral data, explains, "People have hard-wired personality traits and cognitive abilities that are the foundation of everything they do that depends upon thinking, learning or behaving. These strengths are hard-wired, meaning that they are always there. They do not change or go away."

Sound behavioral data answers questions like these:

- Can this person consistently follow the procedures?
- How warm and friendly will they be in people-facing roles?
- Can they manage the actions of others?

Today, there are a few advanced tools that quickly and easily provide this information. Franchising enables people to acquire a proven business model. Behavioral information ensures that the owner has the right people to make their franchise more successful.

As we were building our training company, I was directly involved in launching two psychometric instruments into the Canadian market. I'm a big fan of personality assessments, because they can provide solid behavioral data. This data can be utilized both for gaining deeper insight into how to leverage one's own personality traits and behavior patterns, as well as to understand those of their team members. Several franchisor CEOs also extol the benefits of using personality assessments to gain meaningful and usable behavioral data, so you might consider using a psychometric assessment for yourself and your team to gain insights and map those insights into your performance journey. Of the many assessment tools available, I believe the best are those that measure both behavior and learning capacity.

AWARE-SENSE ZONE 2: INTERNAL, BUSINESS

After you've completed your Zone 1 assessment, you will next assess two types of resources that are available to your business: Intellectual/Conceptual and Physical. This is external to you personally, but still "internal"—think of it as what takes place behind closed doors, or what you and your staff see, but the customer doesn't see:

- Intellectual/Conceptual: Your relationship with your franchisor, and your staff's core skills and motivation levels, their composite of attitudes, and their mindsets. It also includes the intellectual property that your franchisor brings to the equation, whether you use that property or not—things like brand, proven systems and processes, strategic partner-supplier relationships, and the knowledge and experience of your franchisee peers.

- Physical: Your contractual market area or territory of your franchise, as well as your technology, vehicles, production equipment, inventory, facility, cash on hand, and the like. These are your primary resources. For this discussion, "primary resources" are all of the things you need to invest in and develop to provide your customers with an experience that exceeds their expectation, whether it's a product or a service. As Don Elliott, a Great Clips franchisee with fifty-seven salons, says, "You're only going to get out of your business what you're willing to put into it."

Each franchise system has proprietary resources, but generally they fall into these categories:

- Human Resources: Human Resources will be the most important of all primary resources, because it's how well you manage your staff that determines the degree to which you'll achieve your marketing, sales, operations and customer experience goals. Heather Stankard, a Blo Blow Dry Bar franchisee, says, "I'm just really passionate about helping other people and about self-care. That's just very important to me. My number one thing is I value people first."

Ask yourself, how well does my team enable us to meet or exceed our customers' needs in a timely manner? What about meeting any new or expanding needs? To what degree can you add more customers or increase your business volume before you have to invest in more staff, or in improving their skills?

The personality assessments referenced above can be an integral part of your ability to assess the strengths and gaps of your team.

- Financial Resources: Available cash, lines of credit, short-term receivables, etc. Ensuring a steady supply of sufficient financial resources makes most other things possible. Once your business is successfully launched, this steady supply of cash should come from your sales efforts, which are in part driven by your marketing efforts. How well are you managing your cash flow? What about accounts receivable and accounts payable? If your sales are lower, is it a symptom of a bigger problem somewhere else? Does your pricing have enough per-transaction profit margin built in to ensure financial health?

- Intellectual Resources: The franchisor's brand, website, internal systems and processes, marketing and customer engagement strategies, formulas, recipes if you're in the food industry, your customer database, strategic referral and other partnership relationships, customer databases, etc. Which intellectual resources are you using well? Which ones are you not maximizing, or not using at all?

- Physical Resources: Your physical location, machines and equipment, inventory and raw material, vehicles, storage space, etc. Similar questions apply here: How well does your equipment/machinery enable you to fulfill your existing customers' needs in a timely manner? What about meeting those customers' expanded needs? To what degree can you add more customers or increase your business volume before you have to invest in more equipment? Important: when assessing your facility, store or showroom, assess it from three perspectives: through your own eyes, through the eyes of your staff, and through the eyes of your customers.

I would bet heavily that you'll see things differently—things that don't matter to you will be important to your staff; different things will be important to your customers. What your facility looks like sends important signals to others about what you feel is important, or not—what type of message is your facility broadcasting?

- Support Resources: This includes your franchisor's training and support team, your peer franchisees, your Franchisee Advisory Council (if one exists for your system), your franchise and industry associations, your immediate family, and especially coaches and mentors. In my interview with Joel Winters, he put it this way: "Oh man, I can't overemphasize the value of [following the system]. Look, if you're buying a franchise and you're not leveraging that, or the franchisor is not helping you leverage it or making it available, it's a real missed opportunity. For instance, we've been in business two and a half years, but there are certain other locations that have been in business for thirty years, just like Kitchen Tune-Up [the franchisor], and that experience is utterly inaccessible to most [non-franchised] business owners. To not avail yourself of it is ludicrous. We really believe in that, and it's been instrumental in our success."

  Use Survey 3-2 to assess your use of resources.

SURVEY 3-2:
Resources Assessment

On a scale of 1 (very low) to 10 (very high), rate your level of agreement with the following statements.	Minimally 1-4	Moderately 5-7	Highly 8-10
HUMAN RESOURCES			
I have the right number of people to run the business optimally.			
I and my team have the right skillsets to run my business optimally.			
I invest the necessary resources to continually develop my people.			
FINANCIAL RESOURCES			
The business is driving the profit I expect and want.			
The marketing and sales efforts being made by my team and me are driving the revenues I expect.			
Operational and other costs are being well managed and reflect our budgeting and forecasts.			
INTELLECTUAL RESOURCES			
I leverage our brand and the franchisor's marketing strategies to consistently enhance my target customers' awareness of my franchise.			
I leverage my database to stay top-of-mind with potential and past customers.			
I continually update my knowledge of the franchisor's systems and tools available to me and my staff.			

On a scale of 1 (very low) to 10 (very high), rate your level of agreement with the following statements.	Minimally 1-4	Moderately 5-7	Highly 8-10
PHYSICAL RESOURCES			
I ensure that my facility is organized, clean and safe, so that it broadcasts the right message to my clientele and staff.			
My machinery/equipment is well maintained and can accommodate current and next-level growth.			
I maintain sufficient inventory supplies to meet current and imminent orders.			
SUPPORT RESOURCES			
I leverage the franchisor's virtual and in-person training sessions to consistently build my knowledge and capabilities.			
I ensure that my staff leverages the franchisor's virtual and in-person training sessions to consistently build their knowledge and capabilities.			
I regularly seek ways to learn from the experiences and knowledge of my peer franchisees.			
I ensure that my team members regularly seek ways to learn from the experiences and knowledge of their counterparts in my peer franchisees' operations.			
I regularly seek knowledge from other resources, attend conferences, and take courses to sustain my business performance.			

INTERPRETATION: The higher the number, the stronger the indication you are operating in the Performance Zone, or at the top left of the Engagement Zone. To see where your own view differs from that of a trusted source looking in, I recommend that you have:

1. a business coach/mentor also do this survey
2. your key employees also do this survey
3. your spouse/life partner also do this survey

It is my experience that most franchisees only leverage a small fraction of the support resources available to them, which is unfortunate because using those support resources enables them to fully optimize all of their other primary resources. What's encouraging is that this is a relatively easy fix which can yield rapid and substantial progress towards your next-level growth. Making the fix happen, though, will require some additional investment of time, effort and funds.

Which support services are you using well? Which ones are you not maximizing, or not using at all? Which ones can provide immediate impact should you start using them, or use them more effectively?

UTILIZE A KEY PERFORMANCE INDICATOR DASHBOARD

One of the most important components of your Zone 2 instrument panel is your Key Performance Indicator (KPI) dashboard. This is so important that I dedicate an entire chapter to KPIs later in this book. There are a myriad of things that can get measured; it's easy to get lost in the data, or to avoid measuring things altogether. Referring back to the pilot metaphor earlier in the chapter, there are only a handful of KPIs that require regular observation, while others can be visited less frequently. Vanessa Yakobson, CEO of Blo Blow Dry Bar, reveals how beneficial KPIs are to next-level growth:

> Know your numbers and know your benchmarks so that you can really focus in on what levers you can pull. Where are the areas that you should be focusing on to be successful? Zero in on where you can really move the needle for yourself. And once you know what those areas are, manage toward those benchmarks. In other words, know where you're at today and what the benchmark is that you want to achieve. Set interim goals along the way if you need to, so

that you're not putting pressure on yourself to execute on a giant leap that's not realistic based on where you're at today. And then develop an action plan, and really focus in on what the very specific actionable items are and the steps you need to take to get from where you are today to that benchmark or goal.

Use those numbers to make strategic decisions that help you focus on the big opportunities that are really going to move the needle and then translate that into an action plan.

In chapter 8 I will discuss using KPIS to monitor and ensure the ongoing vitality of your business.

AWARE-SENSE ZONE 3: EXTERNAL, LOCAL MARKET OPPORTUNITIES AND FORCES

Now that you have much greater clarity from Zone 1 and Zone 2 assessments of the resources you have at hand to marshal, it's time to start looking outside of your doors at local market opportunities and local market forces. Like primary resources, these local market opportunities and forces will be unique and specific to the type of franchise you bought, so it's best that you work closely with your franchisor's field support team to customize your list of opportunities and forces as much as you can for your specific business. I'll be purposefully general here.

Adam Contos, an entrepreneur, author, and former CEO of RE/ MAX, views this aspect of awareness as being present and active in the community:

If our customers, our franchisees, and our partners don't see us, they won't know that we care. They're going to go with somebody else. So you just can't unlock your door in the morning and go sit in your office in the back of your franchise. It doesn't work that way. You have to communicate with as many people as you can and just care about them. Don't call them and go, "Hey, do you want to buy this?" Call them and go, "Hey, how are you today? I haven't talked to you in a little while. I just want to see how you're doing. Thanks for what you do in our community." And they'll ask the question, "How's your business?" You go, "It's great. I'd love to see you come by one of these days, or is there anything we can bring to you or do you have anybody we can help?" I mean, that's what it boils down to.

LOCAL MARKET OPPORTUNITIES

Ask yourself, "Where can additional revenue come from?" There will be both direct and indirect opportunities; some will require investing in marketing to create awareness and attract attention, while others will require an investment of selling time or networking time. Your location and facility can also be an important business generator, provided the cleanliness and overall customer experience meets or exceeds your visitors' expectations.

Investing in ongoing marketing and sales activities should mostly be focused on customers, whether potential, existing or past; networking time should be primarily focused on building referral networks and strong centers of influence. Take a look at how involved Clara Osterhage is:

> I sit on the boards of the Ohio Chamber of Commerce, the Dayton Chamber of Commerce, and the Ohio chapter of the NFIB [National Federation of Independent Business]; that's probably been one of the most incredibly helpful, wonderful boards that I sit on, because they are really advocating for businesses in Ohio. I also sit on the Ohio Cosmetology and Barber Board.
>
> Now I'm with local people, and I interact with a ton of big businesses in Ohio about local business issues. I believe that being involved and actively seeking to remove obstacles for small businesses and, in particular, the cosmetology industry is critical.
>
> Then there's the national, so I fly into Washington, D.C., every year. In the end, I'm networking with a lot of people who play different roles in business outside of the Great Clips brand.

Complete the following survey to identify how well you're doing in these critical areas, compared to what your franchisor is recommending you do.

SURVEY 3-3:
Marketing Opportunity Assessment

Specific Local Marketing Opportunity	Minimally 1-4	Moderately 5-7	Often 8-10
1. I use SEO, SEM marketing, LinkedIn, Facebook and other social media to advertise my business.			
2. I use traditional marketing (print, radio, billboard, other media) to advertise my business.			
3. I use community marketing to advertise my business: door hangers, yard signs, booths at community events, sports team and other sponsorship, cold calling whether on phone or door-to-door.			
4. I use current technology and applications to attract and interact with my target customers and provide them with a seamless online purchasing experience.			
5. I use my database to reach out to my network: email drip campaigns and announcements to stay in touch with current and past customers, and create potential new customers. I buy target lists (where jurisdictions allow).			
6. I ask for referrals from customers.			
7. I respond to new enquiries in a timely manner (under four hours or next day if overnight).			
8. I use AI auto-text responders for immediate response to inbound enquiries.			
9. I have a high conversion rate of prospective customers (raw leads) into qualified (higher-potential) opportunities.			

Specific Local Marketing Opportunity	Minimally 1-4	Moderately 5-7	Often 8-10
10. I have a high conversion rate for converting qualified opportunities into new clients.			
11. I am increasing sales volumes to existing clients.			
12. I am winning back past clients.			
13. NETWORKING ACTIVITIES:			
• I attend networking events like Chamber of Commerce meetings, joining BNI or other organized networking groups.			
• I create my own networking groups.			
• I build key strategic referral relationships with professionals who are centers of influence.			
• I coach my team on networking activities and hold regular marketing sessions with them.			

Review your survey responses. Which marketing opportunities are providing value and which are not? Do the survey results suggest you need to change your marketing mix to reach more customers?

GROWTH PLAN EXERCISE 3-3
Describe Local Market Forces

Ask yourself what forces are present locally that you have to be mindful of and manage. These could be positive forces that support business growth and next-level change (for example, local population growth means more customers) or negative forces that force you to reconsider some element of your next-level growth objectives (for example, the rerouting of traffic, labor shortages, or tax hikes).

Word of mouth and accumulating lots of positive customer reviews online will be among your biggest driving forces. In retail, anchor tenants are also big driving forces. Innovation trends can also be worth watching, especially where they enhance the customer experience; sometimes this is a local phenomenon, sometimes it's national or even global. Think about how food pick-up/delivery exploded at the start of the pandemic, and how franchisors who innovated with mobile apps evolved rapidly to enhance their customer experience and capture greater market share. So ask yourself, where can increased profit come from? It can come from increasing your sales revenues, or it can come from improving efficiency within your operation, or a combination of both.

- What positive forces are you aware of in your market that may already be benefiting your business?
- What negative forces are you aware of in your market that may already be challenging for your business?

Which of these forces require your highest attention, either to capitalize on opportunity or to mitigate/resolve an existing or imminent challenge?

AWARE-SENSE ZONE 4: EXTERNAL, NATIONAL/
GLOBAL MARKET FORCES

Any business is by definition a global business today. It is exposed to financial threats like inflation and production threats like supply chain and talent shortages, not to mention future pandemic waves, etc. I interviewed Mark Siebert, CEO of iFranchise Group, specifically on national/global market forces that franchisees (and franchisors) should be aware of, and his insight was fascinating. Here are his comments:

ON TREND WATCHING: "I think every business should be looking at macro trends, just in general terms, just trying to figure out how they need to position themselves, because those macro trends will, ultimately, influence different things—the nature of anybody's business. When you're talking about franchising, you're talking about a lot of different industries. What you need to do as a business person [is] you need to be looking at any kind of trend that is going to impact your business in particular."

ON COST OF CAPITAL: "One of the things you want to look at, if you have to borrow money, is cost of capital. As you start looking at things that drive costs of capital, you need to make decisions based on borrowing. You look at those decisions based on, where do you think the interest rate environments are going to be going? What kind of impact will that have on your cost of capital if you've got a variable-based loan?"

ON INFLATION: Inflation is a phenomenon that many of today's franchisees have never had to deal with before. Mark shared an example of a restaurant franchisee who went through a costing exercise early in his business tenure, but hadn't done it again for years, and was perceiving that his food costs had gone way up. Upon deeper analysis, increased product costs and internal theft were part of the issue, but there were other factors. The client shared this with Mark: "My portions are out of control. I don't have good controls over my product. I don't know what my costs really are yet."

In 2022, global supply chain disruptions contributed to increased product, delivery and labor costs in most industries, so it's vital to work closely with your franchisor to keep a close eye on managing supply costs *and* operating costs. Mark has this advice for franchisors and franchisees: "A costing exercise is something you should be doing anyhow, but in an inflationary environment, you need to be doing it more frequently. You need to be aware... and decide whether or not you want to pass along these price increases to your customers."

ON TECHNOLOGY: "Technology's continuing to change things. Technology's continuing to evolve, and if you're not staying on top of macro trends in technology, you're going to find yourself getting left behind as well. This can be something where staying on top of these macro trends is a lot more difficult for someone as an observer of the marketplace, if they're not technologically inclined."

ON LEGISLATIVE CHANGES: "These can certainly have a tremendous impact on what you're doing. Depending on the size of your business, some of the regulations that are out there might impact you as well. Some of the things that might be at play are the laws that govern joint employers, and minimum wage.

"If you're a franchisee operating in multiple markets, and one of those markets is about to raise the minimum wage to fifteen dollars an hour, and you're paying eight dollars, that'd be something you'd want to be keeping your eyes on. Basically, the question that you want to ask yourself is, 'How do any of the economic drivers of the world out there impact [my] business?'"

GROWTH PLAN EXERCISE 3-4
Describe National/Global Market Forces

- What macro trends do you and your franchisor need to be watching?
- What national/global forces are having a positive effect on your business?
- What national/global forces are having a negative effect on your business?
- Which of these forces require your attention, either to capitalize on downstream opportunity, or to mitigate/resolve an anticipated downstream challenge?

GROWTH PLAN EXERCISE 3-5
SWOT Analysis of Market Forces

Based on your answers to the reflection exercise above, complete this SWOT analysis to give you an overall assessment of the forces affecting your business. Update the analysis on a regular basis.

STRENGTHS	WEAKNESSES
OPPORTUNITIES	THREATS

AS JOEL WINTERS EXPLAINS, "It really is important to be aware, because you have to be aware of your financials and your customers and what's going on in the marketplace and how to interact with your franchisor and understanding maybe what people are thinking or feeling." But those are the obvious factors; Joel also understands that awareness is about "having humility and the willingness to be vulnerable, to receive feedback. Assuming positive intent, being flexible; these are all things that lead to or give awareness." And it is the blend of these "soft" skills along with critical thinking and decision-making that are enveloped in a strong aware-sense.

Josh Skolnick, co-founder and CEO of HorsePower Brands, has a more dramatic take on awareness. He says, "Franchisees that are going to be very successful in business will adapt and pivot and change with the times and reinvest in the business. Those who think that the way that they do business today is the way they're going to do business for the next ten years, they're going to die. They are going to fall victim to what I like to call the slow death."

Coupled with your KPIs, the assessments provided in this chapter will become an integral part of the neural network for your business so that you'll have better information faster, which will enable you to consistently achieve your current and next-level desired outcomes.

In the next chapter, we move on to building operational management skills. Please first complete the activities and exercises from this chapter, because the insights you will gain from doing these exercises will transfer into our discussion about leading and managing others.

Driver No. 2 Takeaways

List your top three takeaways from this chapter:

1. _____

2. _____

3. _____

CHAPTER 4

DRIVER NO. 3
Grow Your Operational Management Skills

WE HAVE ALREADY TALKED about a couple of key things in your recipe for success. First, with Driver No. 1 we covered developing a next-level mindset to mentally prepare you to manage the direction of change and growth. Driver No. 2 focused on growing an awareness of the forces at play at a personal and business level. I urge you to revisit the Aware-sense Four-Zone Model to be mindful and reflect about what's working for you and against you, and about what changes you will need to/want to make.

Driver No. 3 is founded on the first two drivers. Sound operational management depends on having the right mindset and constantly reading the signs around you to make the right decisions about how you are running the business. In other words, it is about being execution focused. What does that entail? Graham Weihmiller, chairman and CEO of BNI, offers this insight:

Top performers are really execution focused. Sometimes you have a new franchisee, they want to change the brand overnight. They want to introduce different products or services. Those things may or may not be on the franchisor's roadmap. But the franchisee that is focused on execution of the existing brand is probably going to do better. Now, they should always provide ideas and feedback to the franchisor, and the franchisor ideally is going to involve them in the decision-making process. But I think what is key is that the franchisee understands, at any given point, their primary role is the excellent and consistent execution of the existing model.

Cracking Your Own Performance Code

One of the core foundations of the franchise business model is that the franchisors provide the systems and processes, but leave the day-to-day operational management up to their franchisees. That's the appeal for a lot of people who come to franchising. They don't have to reinvent the wheel or bootstrap a business. They get a system that is expected to make money, provided it is run according to plan with sound operational management. For people who believe they have sound management skills (for example, those who moved from a corporate environment to franchising), it sounds like the perfect deal.

However, unlike corporate employment—where the company's leadership has control over their employees and is responsible for their employees' results—the franchise business model is typically structured so that control, accountability, and responsibility for the day-to-day operations rest with the franchisee. The franchisor does not have control, other than what's defined in the franchise agreement and operations manual; instead, the franchisor exercises influence to encourage their franchisees to execute the various components of their business model.

With so many varieties of business out there, the skills and approaches differ widely, but the following three core premises about management skills can serve as talking points.

Premise 1: Management skills are the combined set of skills that are required to perform the tasks and activities that enable a business to meet and exceed its customers' expectations, while staying true to its vision and purpose.

Premise 2: Robert Katz, an American social and organizational psychologist, stated that there are three types of management skills.[15] When you look at all of the elements you have to manage to run a franchise, reflect on how these skills apply:

- Technical Skills: Technical skills give the managers the ability and the knowledge to use a variety of techniques to achieve their objectives. These skills not only involve operating machines and software, production tools, and pieces of equipment, but also the skills needed to boost sales, design different types of products and services, and market the services and the products.

- Conceptual Skills: These involve the skills managers rely on for abstract thinking and formulating ideas. The manager is able to see an entire concept, analyze and diagnose a problem, and find creative solutions. This helps the manager to effectively predict hurdles their department or the business as a whole may face.

- Human or Interpersonal Skills: These skills represent the manager's ability to interact, work or relate effectively with people. They enable managers to make use of human potential in the company and motivate the employees for better results.

Premise 3: You have to test and work your management skills. For top-performing franchisees, that's essential in striving to be the best in your market.

Before we move on, I want to return to two key discoveries I made in what I call "cracking the performance code." First, anyone, regardless of personality type, skillset, market experience, or business background, can learn how to achieve top performance. They grow into great business owners over time. Second, my research identified a highly consistent set of drivers that a) accelerate next-level growth and higher performance at the franchise ownership level, and b) can be applied across most franchise businesses. Your business is yours to run well, or otherwise. You are not in this alone, but you are accountable for your results. Cracking your own performance code is at the heart of why you bought this book; it begins by assessing and acknowledging your current skill strengths and gaps, then deciding which ones you want to focus on building to the next level.

Seven Key Areas of Operational Excellence

Graham Cooke has a little anecdote about operational excellence that I just love:

> So, you have a franchisee who is struggling, and the regional manager comes in to talk to him about it. The franchisee begins pointing to a lot of externals as to why he's not doing well, and the regional manager says, "Well, the first thing we're going to do is drive down to the hardware store and buy a can of black paint, and we're going to come back and paint your windows so you can't see outside of them." Franchisees need to start fixing their business from the inside out. Very often, if a franchisee is blaming external factors, he's kind of taking himself out of the equation.
>
> Even though they bought a system, it all begins with them. We talked about hard work and positive energy, but in the end they still have to make it go every day. The system won't run itself. And, when things go badly, the best franchisees dig in and look in the mirror and are introspective about what they can do.

While you may have studied the manuals to the point of being able to quote passages over Sunday dinner (to the delight of your family, I'm sure), you must understand what's behind the curtain—in other words, knowing the business drivers of the model. The success of your business rests on optimally managing these drivers. It takes self-awareness to say, "I am not managing this driver as well as I should be, so I need to take action to close the gap."

The same awareness extends to every member of your team. Here are the seven key areas of operational management:
- customer acquisition (marketing and sales)
- production
- delivery/fulfillment
- human resources/staffing
- financial management
- facilities and equipment maintenance
- safety and security

> You might be asking, "What about technology?" Technology is more of an enabler and amplifier that can make processes more efficient. Always look for ways technology can improve efficiencies and lower costs.

What proficiencies are lacking? Explore this by asking these three questions:
1. What is your current level of knowledge of the systems, and what is the team's?
2. How would you describe your level of engagement in the business, and the team's level of engagement, and what does this reveal for you?
3. What results are you and your team seeing, and how does your performance stack up against the franchisor's KPI system averages?

THE CUSTOMER ACQUISITION PROCESS

It is a truism that it is not the franchisor's job to deliver customers to your doorstep. It's not like building bleachers and a baseball diamond in a field. No, the customers won't come. Keeping customers and finding new ones is up to you. You have the business, the training, and either some or a lot of business savvy. It is your responsibility to execute those systems, one of which is sales and marketing.

The franchisor can do everything right regarding marketing and branding, but if the franchisee cannot deliver on the brand's promised experience for the customer, and if they do not teach their team members to consistently deliver a good experience, sales will be subpar. Attracting, gaining and retaining your customers is one of the earliest and most critical business drivers to master, whether you're directly responsible for doing it or you hire and oversee someone to do it.

Why? Because "nothing happens until someone sells something," according to Arthur H. "Red" Motley, a former president of the US Chamber of Commerce and publisher of *Parade* magazine who was recognized as one of the greatest salesmen of the 20th century.[16]

Here's what Colin Bates, a multi-market regional developer of Jan-Pro of Canada, has to say about business retention and sales: "We know what the levers are for growth in the business. That's our prime objective—growth. You've got to have customer retention. You've got to have sales. You have to have those two working in unison. It's not enough that you can sell remarkable amounts with it all going out the back door. You have to have both pieces working. Then you have to be able to collect on the bills as well. You've got to do that in a timely fashion."

To get customers to the point of purchase, your marketing has to work. You have to motivate the customer to want to do business with you. This means beating the competition by amplifying your presence in the local market and community.

Adam Contos told me, "The first thing is, the top performers are good people. They want to help people do the right thing in their franchise. And this is important, as part of their community. I mean, a franchise is synonymous with community. And if somebody thinks that they're just going to buy a store and plant it someplace and not become part of that community, they're not going to be successful. So you have to be a good person and a good partner and member of the community. The community expects you to show up. And when you show up for them, they show up for you."

It's about how you create awareness of your company in your local market, and then build that awareness to generate curiosity and interest. Once built, then it's about getting the potential customer to take action and engage your company on some level.

Many franchisors will invest their marketing fund in brand-building initiatives regionally and nationally, and will oversee and manage the websites, social media posts, news stories, central databases, etc. The franchisee must focus on and execute the activities that will drive business in their local market. Activities include networking, local market ad spending, and actively engaging their community through sponsorships. Please complete the survey below to benchmark your sales process and see where there is room for improvement.

SURVEY 4-1:
Customer Engagement and Sales Process Assessment

This is a general sales process, so customize as needed to reflect the specific components of your business. "Customer" includes prospective, current and returning customers.

On a scale of 1 (very low) to 10 (very high), rate your level of agreement with the following statements.	Minimally 1-4	Moderately 5-7	Exceptionally 8-10
LEAD ENGAGEMENT AND QUALIFICATION			
I have given select team members the role of driving customer engagement, by utilizing our various media channels.			
I work closely with my team to improve customer relations skills.			
I engage with customers and drive best practices in customer service with my team.			
NEEDS ASSESSMENT AND PROBLEM SOLVING			
My team understands what a "needs assessment" is and can apply it to our business. My team knows how to use it to create solutions for the customer.			

On a scale of 1 (very low) to 10 (very high), rate your level of agreement with the following statements.	Minimally 1-4	Moderately 5-7	Exceptionally 8-10
I have confidence in my team to respond quickly to customer questions and concerns. They do not need my input unless a very serious situation needs my attention.			
I invest in sales-related skills development for my team, at least annually.			
SOLUTION PRESENTED—ASK FOR THE ORDER			
My team is trained on how to move from ensuring a customer has clarity on a solution to "closing," which is asking for the order.			
If a customer is hesitant, my team knows which questions to ask to maintain the focus of the customer and provide the right solution.			
We maintain and update a history of interactions with our customers.			
ORDER IS CONFIRMED			
Once a client has confirmed an order, we have a clear and efficient internal process to move the order through to delivery.			
We have a flexible production schedule to ensure quantity and size of orders outside the norm can be fulfilled.			
We keep the customer informed every step of the way.			

On a scale of 1 (very low) to 10 (very high), rate your level of agreement with the following statements.	Minimally 1-4	Moderately 5-7	Exceptionally 8-10
QUALITY CONTROL			
We have quality control checks at various points.			
We never ship an order that is in any way inferior to our best work.			
We regularly seek ways to learn from the experiences and knowledge of other franchisees to improve our quality control process.			
REFERRALS AND REPEAT BUSINESS			
The team follows up with the customer upon delivery. Any concerns the customer has are immediately addressed.			
We ask for reviews and referrals in our customer follow-up.			
We engage our customers on a regular basis, even if they are not ordering anytime soon.			

NOTE: Adapt the survey questions to your business. Add questions. Look for gaps in the way you engage with customers and lead them through the customer experience journey. Always look for ways to improve that journey.

CUSTOMER ENGAGEMENT FOR DIFFERENT TYPES OF BUSINESSES
Your sales process will depend on the type of franchise you are running. For example:

· For inbound-driven businesses like retail shops and restaurants, the selling starts when someone walks through the door. The customer is likely familiar with your offerings, so your staff must be prepared for that customer-facing moment to get them to buy on the spot.

- For mobile businesses like home improvement or residential cleaning, prospective customers find you through an online search or by taking notice of your marketing efforts, and then contact you, by phone or email. So these businesses are also in the "inbound" category. As with other inbound businesses, the potential customer is likely aware of your offerings. Your staff proceeds to arrange for an in-home visit to meet with the prospective customer to do the needs assessment and provide a quote. Then, of course, comes the "ask" for an order.

- For outbound businesses like commercial services or consulting, this sector typically has the most complex selling process, likely starting with outbound phone calls and in-person cold calls where you have to initiate contact. Your potential customers are unlikely to be familiar with your service offering, so you or your staff will first have to find out who the decision-maker is, and find out how to get them to accept an appointment with you.

Regardless of whether your business is inbound, mobile or outbound, your franchisor has developed a sales-and-marketing track for you and your staff to run on. The more you and your customer-facing team build their selling skills, the richer the opportunity for selling.

Your success is connected to your ability to deliver on the brand promise. In the words of Adam Contos, the happiest of the RE/MAX family members are those who...

> ...have a deep sense of ownership in the brand. They're not using "our" brand. They make the brand "their own," and they're in love with it because it's their "brand." And they're the first ones to step up and speak for the brand, defend the brand, enhance the brand, protect the brand. You know, ultimately it comes down to this: you want to build [a sense of] ownership in your franchisees, and when they build ownership, they become connected, and they're the happiest because they understand there's no perfect world out there. And those are the ones who are proud of wearing the jersey that

they're wearing on their team. They're not just there to make a buck. They're there to make a difference.

We have to get up every day, open our eyes and go fight the battle in order to grow our businesses.

PRODUCTION

Once the customer has said "yes" to making a purchase, the production process kicks in. This includes inventory sourcing and control, equipment and machinery utilization, staff utilization, production and finishing, quality control, and output level expectations (KPIs).

In businesses like printing and signage, the production process is largely the custom manufacturing of the products. In the food industry, it's the prepping and cooking of food. In service industries, it's the appointment scheduling and preparation for fulfillment by skilled technicians (installers, repair technicians, hair stylists, registered massage therapists, mechanics, pet walkers, etc.).

Is the production aspect linked to customer experience? You bet. A machine that breaks down, a lack of inventory, poor quality control, and unnecessary delays all contribute to customer dissatisfaction.

What is the process you use to oversee production on your team? How frequently do you meet with them to discuss production goals and performance against KPIs?

It is your responsibility and the team's to ensure that the standards you operate by are met and even exceeded. Look at how Doug Brauer, a TPF with FASTSIGNS, ensures optimum production capability: "Every morning, we have a work-start meeting that starts at eight and it goes for fifteen minutes and in fifteen minutes, it's over. Everybody walks out of there and they know what their goals are for that day, what they have to do. And they work as a team to make sure it's achieved."

DELIVERY/FULFILLMENT

In delivering your product or service, you have the opportunity to exceed the customer's expectations. This is where the customer experience lives; it's where the franchisee's production efforts intersect with the customer's expectations. At every interaction with your business, the customer is assessing their overall experience, and the degree to which their expectations have or have not been met.

Some product-based businesses have a simpler delivery model; for example, where it's a straightforward drop-off or pick-up scenario for the customer and there's minimal interaction. For retail product stores, the on-floor staff's behavior is pivotal in determining what the customer's shopping experience will be. Service-based businesses require substantially more interaction with the customer, and some demand very high levels of customer attentiveness. In the words of Joel Winters at Kitchen Tune-Up,

> Kitchen Tune-Up has customer service trust points, things that we promise to customers that we're going to do, and we live by those, and [they're] embedded in our team's culture as well. We show up on time, we communicate, we clean up after ourselves daily. There's a lot of these things that you can say you do, and maybe some people say it, but we actually do those things, and we think it makes an impact. We've got a massive number of Google reviews for the short two and a half years we've been in business, and they're all five stars, and people like working with us. We set that expectation from the outset.

Many franchisees think that "if my team makes a good product or provides a good service, then I've met the customer's expectations." Maybe they have on the actual product, but what about the rest of the customer's experience? Product or service delivery is an important component of fulfillment, but there are other parts that are equally important. What are the parts of your customer's experience that you might not be seeing? When was the last time you looked at the experience you provide through the customer's eye? An important exercise for any franchisee is to occasionally map the customer's journey to look for ways to improve their experience, or to find points of friction or lack of attention.

Think about when the customer...

- goes into a restaurant and the bathroom is dirty. Might they extrapolate that the kitchen is also dirty?
- goes into a paint store and there's a noticeable scratch in the drywall.
- is expecting the service crew to arrive at a specific time, but they arrive an hour late.

Each franchise system has its own delivery and fulfillment methodologies, which form a core element of the franchisor's business systems that every franchisee should master. What are yours?

MANAGING YOUR TALENT

There are several components to managing your team; in the next chapter we'll focus on the leadership aspects. From an operational management perspective, what are the systems you use to drive optimal performance and support your team? How structured is your hiring process?

- Do you have the same base of interview questions for each candidate?

- Do you do background checks if required and check references?

- Do you use behavioral data (personality assessments) as part of your hiring process to screen your prospective employees? You might be thinking, "I'm already short-staffed. I wish I had the problem of needing to screen employees, but I'll take who I can get!" Well, the true benefit of using good assessment tools shows up after you hire someone.

- How structured is your new employee onboarding process? Do you have a new employee onboarding or orientation manual? If so, how current is it?

- How frequently do you conduct performance reviews? What criteria do you use to measure performance?

There are too many important components of talent management support to capture here. What's important is that you look to your franchisor and your peer franchisees to learn more about how to use the talent management tools available to you through your franchise system.

Here's how franchisee Cynthia Keenan merges sound process and clear communication to drive strong team performance:

> Every new employee not only gets the handbook, I sit down with each one of them and tell them what the expectations are, and how we deal with things when we go astray. The bottom line is I respect them as the professionals that they are—we're all adults. I'm going to spit out all this information to you, but you're a professional, you're an adult, and I trust that you're going to be able to follow these rules. And when you don't, there will be consequences and I will follow up on them.
>
> With all of these rules and everything else I always boil it down to one thing: work hard and be nice to people. [If you do that] everything else falls in place.

You are responsible for training your staff well and looking after them. Not everyone who comes through your door looking for a job will be a straight-A student or exuding confidence. There are diamonds in the rough. Hire for empathy and attitude. You can always teach skills, as Colin Bates emphasized:

> When we hire here, we want to make sure the character of an individual is in alignment with what we're trying to do here. We look for skills too. If you demonstrate the ability to learn the skills any day of the week, I'm going to take character over skills and make sure I've got the qualities and people that we're looking for. We can train the rest. I spend quite a bit of time on coaching and development with our folks. I just don't think you can ever do too much of that stuff.

When it comes to a philosophy about managing your human capital, which is a fancy way of saying managing your team, how much thought do you give to the quality of life of your employees? Values matter and are the connective tissue between you, staff and customer.

Invest in your team. Steve White, president and COO of Puro-Clean, says, "The top performers are people who understand 'team.' They are people who invest in their business. They don't just invest financially. Everybody does that when they start, but you keep investing. You reinvest in that business. And more importantly, you invest in relationships with your team in your local marketplace, with key customer groups and people groups like that."

KNOW YOUR FINANCIALS

A recurring theme in the interviews I conducted is that you have to know your financials. A good franchisor will train on the numbers, recognizing that franchisees have varying degrees of financial literacy. Let's hear some perspectives on the numbers and what metrics top-performing franchisees pay attention to.

John Prittie, CEO of Two Men and a Truck Canada, says the top performers set goals that are measured by financials:

> They put action plans in place. And they include the team in the process because they have to get the buy-ins, right? Top performers inspect financials to see if expectations are being met. They're always looking at the data, the KPIs, and hold people responsible and accountable. [They] understand the value of reports and data. And these guys always have timely financial statements as well. It's amazing. The bottom performers are the last ones to file their financial statements and tax returns with us.

Steve White has a mantra: "Know your numbers." He says, "[People] who run their business by the numbers have a good command of them. The greater command you have of your numbers, the greater your level of confidence will be in decision-making. The more quickly you make good decisions, this can keep your business growing."

PuroClean helps its franchise owners know their numbers. Steve comments, "We teach field support people how to assess an anonymous set of financials. They don't know who the business belongs to. They will go through those financials and tell me if they are going to have a meeting with the franchisee who owns this business. They need to be able to identify what the top three things are that they want to talk to the franchisee about operationally, based on what they saw in the financials."

This level of engagement by PuroClean speaks volumes about awareness. The franchisor has awareness of the operational performance of the franchises, and builds awareness of the success factors in the franchisee base.

Ned Lyerly, CEO of CKE Restaurants (Hardee's and Carl's Jr.), which has a global footprint of over 3,900 franchised or company-operated restaurants, talked about having his finger on the pulse of the franchisees' financials:

> As a franchisor, we know that some franchisors and franchisees know their financials like the back of their hand. It's the transparency and visibility to sales, P&L and balance sheet reporting that is important.
>
> Franchisees that are large and others that want to grow may not have as much financial wind under their wings as they need to in order to go forward, because their balance sheets are a little stretched. If there's transparency and knowledge and partnership, we can work together to find out how we can accommodate growth. We want them to grow. They want to grow. And growth's part of their solution to be in a better financial position. So it's really navigating through this sort of situation that I find interesting.

The key words Ned uses about the relationship between franchisor and franchisee are "transparency and knowledge and partnership." The numbers tell a story about the financial health of the franchisee. Transparency can help identify financial challenges and working together can help solve them and set goals to grow the business.

Dave Mortensen, president of Anytime Fitness and Self Esteem Brands, talks about mastering financial management: "Know your numbers. Top performers have a financial fluency in the business. They understand it. Top-performing franchisees are very astute in their numbers."

Dave adds that top franchisees "know their lead measures, and they're going to know their lagging measures. When they look for real estate, they don't get emotional about it. They're going to know the numbers that drive the business. They're going to know the densities of their population. They're going to know what EBITDA [earnings before interest, taxes, depreciation, and amortization] means. They're going to know all those key metrics to drive their business performance."

Knowing your numbers is the baseline to operating well and opening the door to future growth. If you feel you're not strong here, you're not alone. The reality is that most people who become franchisees do not come from a financial background, and find this aspect of their business very intimidating, so they don't pay enough attention to this vital information. In chapter 8 we'll do a deep dive into KPIs to help you make better sense of this critical data; financial KPIs are an important part of the KPI data set.

FACILITIES AND EQUIPMENT MAINTENANCE

Maintaining your facility well is a reflection of values and respect for customers and staff. A clean, well-lit and well-organized environment shows you care about your business. I've seen some businesses where the customer area is impeccable, but the back office and staff areas are in disarray. This is a confusing message to your staff, suggesting that maybe they matter less than the customer.

TPFs know that facility and equipment maintenance is an important part of how well their team members are able to perform their duties, and an important part of the overall message TPFs strive to communicate to staff and customers alike—that whoever comes into this facility is important. For mobile businesses, this extends to the condition of their vehicles and the way their employees behave on the roads. Take a few minutes to walk through your business as if you were giving your most important customer a tour. Try looking at your facility, machinery, equipment, vehicles, and so on through their eyes. Identify which facilities need some attention and care.

SAFETY AND SECURITY

Safety protocols should be a part of every business; this includes customer safety and proper storage of perishables and toxic chemicals. It includes staff safety through training and monitoring proper use of tools and equipment, handling of materials, etc. It also includes having good security systems that protect your facilities and staff from break-ins. Train your staff on how to avoid putting themselves and your customers and business at risk. Follow the system manuals and make sure safety protocols are understood and rehearsed.

Views on Operational Excellence

Graham Cooke of A&W focuses on a number of areas of excellence he expects from franchisees, and two of these are "operational mastery of the basics" and "financial management." A&W, like other good franchise systems, has operational processes in place that are tried, proven and adaptable. It is the franchisee's responsibility and obligation to learn and rigorously apply these processes.

The interviewees made it clear that operational mastery is not possible without engagement from the top and from the team. John Prittie says,

> When everybody is aligned on their goals and their objectives, and comes to work happy and wanting to contribute, and wanting to support each other—when I walk into those franchises, I go like,

"Wow, this is a happy place." And somebody makes a sale, and there's the high fives. And guys get back from the field after doing a big move and they got some nice tips and the customers are very happy, so high fives all around. They just have teams that just love working together, and they feed off each other's energy and enthusiasm.

I want to close this chapter with the hard-won wisdom of a consummate franchisor. He's like the Wayne Gretzky of franchising. His name is Jack Lapointe, and he is the founder of Jan-Pro, the world's largest commercial cleaning franchise. What was the most critical thing he had to learn about building the business? Jack says,

> I learned to overcome the barriers that held us back from being the best brand we could be. Over those years, I learned how to create the level of success we desired. It started with developing a team of professionals who knew the techniques that would allow us to accomplish more each day than most of our competitors. At the same time, we applied those techniques with a leadership approach that would drive a profound amount of positive influence with our franchise owners and business community.
>
> And, of course, there's the Jan-Pro culture, and it's simple: it's an organization where teamwork, loyalty and communication are the norm rather than the exception. Everyone contributes, whether it is best practices or anything else—and everyone thrives. This is a culture where this attitude continually impacts our level of success!

To manage the business optimally, Jan-Pro had to be a company that was open to learning all the time and improving the business. Have the right people on the bus. Believe in the system and the way of doing things. Grow leadership capability, which we'll elaborate on in the next chapter. Make sure everyone thrives.

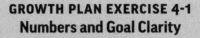

GROWTH PLAN EXERCISE 4-1
Numbers and Goal Clarity

Reflect on the following excerpt from my interview with franchisee Heather Stankard about how she works with numbers and sets goals. Is your process similar or different? What changes can you make to get closer to mastery over the numbers and your operation?

> Every two weeks I put in my goals for the following two weeks, and I have goals for my numbers as well, like 'This is the retail [product sales goal] I want to meet. This is how many blowouts [hair styling appointments] I want to do. This is how many members I want to get, and this is how much I want to spend on marketing.' It's for every little category.
>
> I take the time to sit down and write down my numbers, because if you don't know your numbers, you're not going to be as successful as you can be. You must know your numbers. So, by doing this, it's twofold. I get to know my numbers better, but I also get to find different ways to achieve my goals, to achieving even higher goals. It's very productive for me.

Driver No. 3 Takeaways

List your top three takeaways from this chapter:

1. _____
2. _____
3. _____

CHAPTER 5

DRIVER NO. 4
Grow Your People

IN MY INTERVIEW with Angela Brown, she made a point of differentiating management from leadership. She explained that management is "getting people to do what they ought to do," whereas "leadership is next level—it's where you inspire people to do things they never thought were possible. It takes a little bit of extra effort and time on your part as a leader, but it's so rewarding. You have to be intentional—you can't wing it. Every conversation with every client, and every team member, matters."

In this chapter we'll help you see why growing your people is critical to achieving next-level growth. Along the way, you will become a better leader. As I emphasized in the last chapter, operational management skills and leadership skills are closely linked. How well you apply them in tandem will directly influence the results your business experiences. As your business grows, it's imperative that you grow your people by helping them master the work you need them to do. You'll hear numerous voices in this chapter that emphasize letting go of control and trusting people to get things done. Vanessa Yakobson views trust as essential to the culture of her company:

I think top performers do an amazing job of building team culture, and getting their teams to work together in a way where the teams come to trust each other because they like each other [and] they consider each other friends. So how do you do that as the leader? You create those opportunities for your team to come together socially. You create those opportunities for them to come together in a work context, bring them together for brainstorming, for opportunities to learn from one another. And I think that the franchise partners that do that successfully, do that because they're able to be part of that mix.

You want to be there for your team, you want to develop those personal connections and you want to create those opportunities for your team members to develop the personal connections among them... If your team members consider each other to be friends, that way they can trust each other and rely on each other in the context of your business.

I especially took notice of how Vanessa talked about creating opportunities and a learning environment. Adam Contos would agree with Vanessa: "The top franchisees are passionate leaders who don't feel that it's a position, they feel that it's an action. They exemplify the behavior and standards that they expect from their people. They model what they need to see in their organizations. They don't just ask people to do it."

What I find especially interesting about Adam's take on leadership is "they don't just ask people to do it." In other words, top franchisees model exemplary leadership because they expect their people to be leaders too. As you prepare to learn more about leadership, pause for a moment and take a baseline reading of a few of your current leadership patterns. If you were asked in a few sentences to describe what your current leadership style is, how would you answer? Think about how you would answer the following questions:

- How effectively are you creating opportunities for your people to excel and grow?

- In what ways are you setting them up for success by building the right environment?
- How often do you acknowledge their contributions as meaningful in moving the business forward?

At the end of the chapter you will find an exercise and survey that will give you a more rounded assessment of your leadership style.

In the previous chapter we talked about a winning culture in terms of operational management. This chapter will break down leadership capabilities as defined by franchisees and franchisors so that you get a perspective on leadership in action and can identify where it's important to start adapting your own leadership approach.

The Ingredients of a Winning Culture

LEADERSHIP STYLES

There are too many styles and methodologies of leadership to claim that any one style is the best one. Let's mention just a few of the more common ones.

There's the autocratic command-and-control leader who hoards control and makes all the decisions. There's the collaborative leader who gets people's input and suggestions, then makes the decisions and gives their people some operational latitude regarding how things get done. There's even the consensus-driven leader who gives everyone a vote in what should get done and how. No one style is "best," as each has its pros and cons. Also, the leader's personality has to be congruent with the style they seek to deploy.

"Situational leadership" is one of the more practical styles, where the specific situation influences the style of leadership required. Two main bodies of thought are available on this and it is advisable that you study them. One is Paul Hersey and Ken Blanchard's Situational Leadership Theory, and the other is the Goleman Theory of Situational Leadership, by Daniel Goleman, author of the renowned book *Emotional Intelligence.*

Mary Thompson, COO of Neighborly, sees her company as a "leadership incubator." Franchisees receive basic training, including a class called Leading with Purpose on Purpose. Mary says,

> What does leadership look like? Not just pie in the sky, but what actions are you going to do on a day in and day out basis that allow you to practice leadership? The strong leaders recruit better people. The strong leaders retain the strongest people. The strong leaders move their organization faster. The strong leaders have happier workforces, and they're generally happier as well.
>
> And so I hear all the time, "Well, that person, I'm not so sure what kind of leader they can or will be." Leadership is a taught skill. Do you have some people that are more natural at it than others? Yes, but it's just like some kids learned to walk earlier than other kids, but it is something you need to practice all the time.

Three takeaways from Mary's thought leadership I want to highlight are:

1. Leadership is a taught skill.
2. The strong leaders retain the strongest people and have happier workforces. What are the keys to a happy team? At a minimum these are recognition and reward, mutual respect, a safe working environment, wellness programs, and work/life balance.
3. The strong leaders move their organization faster.

....

"Leadership is a taught skill" does not mean the teaching solely rests on someone else to teach you. While that is part of the equation, great leaders are also constantly in a state of self-education: "What can I improve next? Where can I get the next bit of information to improve in _____ area?"

....

Many of the top-performing franchisees and franchisor CEOs I interviewed make their values visible so that the team is always reminded of the leadership behaviors they should be modeling.

My personal belief is that the pinnacle of leadership style, skill and capability is *servant leadership*. Time and time again during my research servant leadership was identified as a preferred leadership style, and many interviewees mentioned it as their preference. So, what the heck is servant leadership?

While it is a timeless concept, the phrase "servant leadership" was coined by Robert K. Greenleaf, founder of the Greenleaf Center for Servant Leadership, in an essay that he published in 1970. Greenleaf wrote:

> A servant leader focuses primarily on the growth and well-being of people and the communities to which they belong. While traditional leadership generally involves the accumulation and exercise of power by one at the "top of the pyramid," servant leadership is different. The servant leader shares power, puts the needs of others first, and helps people develop and perform as highly as possible.[17]

I love how Greenleaf refers to the "shadings and blends that are part of the infinite variety of human nature." You could say that Greenleaf was way ahead of his time. Because today we recognize inclusion and diversity as essential elements to the growth and development of our teams and organizations.

EVERYONE IS ON THEIR OWN GROWTH JOURNEY

Just as you are on your own growth journey, so is every one of your employees. Whether you want it or not, you have a direct ability to influence the quality and trajectory of that journey for each of your employees. People make decisions about where they'll work based on how much they feel their needs are being met in the job. It's not just about the money; there are other motivators like time flexibility and the work environment that need to be considered.

Today's employee pool includes people from four generations—boomers, Gen X, millennials, and Gen Z. Each group sees the workplace differently, but rarely are wages at the top of the "why I work here" list. In his book *Drive*, Daniel Pink gets at what's really important to workers after money is taken out of the equation. When I consider all of the insights I heard from TPFs and franchisor CEOs, it's no surprise that Pink's three top motivating factors are purpose, mastery, and autonomy.[18] All of these are progressive stages of the growth journey.

Let's not completely discount the traditional power-based leadership practices that have shaped the workplace, because those controlling and directing styles do get results. Employees' expectations of the workplace and what they want from their jobs is evolving though, and the more effectively you can lead your people by inspiring them as we've discussed here, instead of by controlling and directing them, the more those employees will want to stay around, and want to contribute and delight you by exceeding your expectations.

So, as you look at how you contribute to your employees' growth journey, it's important to ask yourself what leadership style you are using and to what degree that style is getting the results you are seeking to achieve. Look at your business through your employees' eyes and ask why people should work for you. What can keep them coming back, and keep them performing at levels that enable you to achieve your own financial and lifestyle goals?

....

"Clients do not come first. Employees come first. If you take care of your employees, they will take care of the clients." RICHARD BRANSON

"Always treat your employees exactly as you want them to treat your best customers." STEPHEN COVEY

....

So many franchisees and independent business owners invest tremendous time and money to find new paying customers and convert them into repeat customers, only to lose them because of less-than-stellar experience with the staff. This is far less likely when you treat your team members as your most important repeat customer—because that's exactly what they are.

The most unpleasant people to work for see their employees as a resource to be exploited and consumed, while the best people to work for see their employees as their most important customers to be served. Reflect deeply on where you really are on this continuum. Are you exploiting or empowering your employees? How are you contributing to their growth journey? How engaged are they?

Websites like GlassDoor.com make it transparent for people to find great work environments and depart from the less desirable environments they might be stuck in. So I'll say it again: Look at your workplace through your employees' eyes. Is yours one that people would want to join, or leave?

When I discussed the performance journey in chapter 3, it was in the context of where franchisees are on their journey. Well, this applies equally to employees who work for you, with one big difference—they do not have the foundational motivator of being their own boss that brought you to business ownership, so it behooves you to understand what drives your people and what can keep them engaged—and it's different for every one of them.

Some of you are thinking about the members of your team and wishing in Technicolor that you could delegate to more of them and give them more responsibility, allowing them to prove their potential. And maybe you can; it might be in how you approach doing so. Sam Reges, a large multi-unit franchisee of Great Clips, puts accountability squarely on the shoulders of her people. She says that her managers . . .

> . . . don't get to say "the company did this or the company did that." You're a manager in the company. So figure out how to take responsibility and explain it in a way that your staff can understand. We aren't just doing this because the company said so. We are doing this because this is what it's going to do for us. This is what we're going to gain from it. This is how we're going to fix this problem or identify this other thing. You have to take ownership in that.

I think sometimes it's so easy for people, in any business, any job, to say, "Oh, well, my owner said I have to do this." I'm like, "Stop it. That's not gaining you anything. It's not getting you anywhere. It's in fact probably taking away respect from you, because you look like you don't agree with it." And I think that's something that causes people so many problems; they blame the franchisor or blame the whatever. No one gains anything by doing that.

The reality is that you likely have employees performing at varying levels. While some are engaged, others are just "showing up" and it's really hard to get them to do what you need them to do. Refer back to page 55 and think for a moment. Do you have employees in the Mediocrity Zone and haven't figured out how to guide them into the Engagement Zone? I can assure you that the less engaged they are, the more they are looking for a way out—instead of a way up. A natural progression is that some of them can become your future managers, who in turn ignite the employees they oversee, with the same skillset and leadership style you nurture in them.

ENGAGEMENT AND GROWTH

Leading means helping your people see their "way up." Angela Brown lives by this principle:

It's about engaging them and making them feel like their individual goals and desires are important. It's not just about the business; they don't get up every morning thinking, "I'm going to go out there and make that franchise the best it can be today." That's not why they get up and come in and want to crush it. There's other personal reasons why they want to go out and crush it every day. It's up to us as the leaders, the franchise owners, to become intimately familiar with what those reasons are and then connect the dots for them.

The next-level mindset applies to you just as it applies to your people—the more effectively you help your people grow, the more engaged they will be, and the more you'll reap both tangible and intangible rewards. Going back to Angela's comment, the more you understand what's important to each of your employees, and help them connect those dots, the more successful your business will become. And in the hypercompetitive market for employees, how well you accomplish this will directly impact how well you'll be able to find, and keep, great employees.

If you're still skeptical, check out a 2017 white paper[19] (a four-minute read) on employee engagement by motivationWorks, a culture-building platform that empowers people to thrive in the workplace. This paper, based on a Gallup survey, is one of the most succinct and effective papers I've read on understanding motivational factors and has some stunning data about how important motivation and engagement are in our current workforce. For instance, fulfilled employees experience:

- 35% higher productivity in their positions
- 99% greater loyalty to their company
- 55% more creativity in their daily tasks
- 85% more satisfaction with their daily tasks
- 61% more willingness to go the extra mile
- 106% more willingness to turn down another job for more money (Wow!)
- 114% greater engagement overall

Fast-forward to 2022, where several in-depth studies about the emerging "quiet quitting" phenomenon are underway. The debate rages on about what this movement is all about; I subscribe to the psychologists and HR professionals who believe that a core component of people's decisions to quietly quit is a lack of engagement in their jobs.

It might be stating the obvious, but a critical aspect of your leadership is to provide meaningful work for your employees, make sure the work environment is safe, and encourage the exchange of ideas. Using behavioral data to ensure effective alignment of roles and duties to behavioral traits helps to set your employees up for greater success and fulfillment.

From a franchisor's perspective, Keith Gerson, president of franchise operations for FranConnect, offers findings from the efforts of two consulting firms (Higher Logic and Ingage Consulting) that collaborated on a study on engagement, identifying what the different traits were and how those traits were represented among the top quartile of franchisees versus the bottom quartile, and just how great of a chasm that was.

> The thing that I think is most important of all is engagement. Engaged franchisees were 3.7 times more profitable than those who were identified as non-engaged. Those that were engaged [at] a high level had a 19 percent increase in operating income, while those with a low level of engagement had a 13 percent decrease in operating income.
>
> It was also, I think, a revelation to note that all engaged franchisees recommended the system. Forty-six percent of non-engaged franchisees don't recommend their brand... And that's why I think that engagement is really the greatest predictor of success of any of the [leadership] behaviors.

MINDSET, SKILLSET, AND ACTIVITY

Jason Zickerman, president and CEO of The Alternative Board, provided these insights into what top performers have:

> I always tell franchisees that there's three parts to the success equation: mindset, skillset, and activity. Those are the three components that build success. Without any one of them in the equation, it becomes like pushing a boulder uphill. Whenever I look at someone who is a high performer, it's because they have all three parts of the success equation in action. They have a great mindset. Even though we offer much support, at the end of the day it is on them to execute. So they have to have that business-mind mentality of "It's up to me."
>
> They have a skillset to learn something new, to commit, to becoming excellent, and to be committed to becoming better, which is mission critical.
>
> So that activity of doing the right things, being in front and following the process—that activity has gotten the system to where it

is today. I think that's a very important thing. And I guess it's those people who are confident enough in themselves to know that they could be humble enough to not feel that they don't know everything and there's a learning curve to be had.

As Jason says, the success equation requires mindset and skills, and taking action. Action requires confidence and also vulnerability. The good leader can admit to not knowing everything and be on a learning curve just as much as their team members are on a learning curve. Angela Brown supports Jason's perspective:

> Be true to yourself, be honest with yourself, and know that it's okay if you don't know everything. Vulnerability is one of the key areas of success for most people—just learning to be vulnerable and knowing that it's okay not to have all the answers. Especially as a leader, we think that we have to be the guru of everything, but we don't. And then again, permission for people around you to make mistakes, because that's when the gates of creativity open up for everyone to help the business, but also, the trust factor kicks in, because without trust you have nothing.

Servant Leadership in the Community

I respect how Greenleaf acknowledges, "A servant leader focuses primarily on the growth and well-being of people and the communities to which they belong." I've already referenced several quotes from TPFs and franchisor CEOs about the importance of being involved in your community, so let's look for a moment at a few of the communities you have the opportunity to serve, for each represents fertile soil to be cultivated:

- the immediate geographic community around your business, where your customers exist
- the recreational communities your customers are a part of (think hobbies, kids' sports, etc.)
- the business community that you're a part of, where other businesses (both noncompetitive and competitive) build

relationships with the same types of customers that you have and want
- your faith community: the subject of faith and serving a higher power came up as a core value and purpose in several TPF interviews
- the community of peer franchisees that your franchisor has built
- the two immediate communities you've been building through your business:
    - the community of your paying customers, and
    - the community of your team within the four walls of your business

SERVANT LEADERSHIP IN THE BUSINESS

THE EMPLOYEES

What my research revealed about top performers is the care they take with their people. This includes high standards in training, wellness programs, proper pay and incentives, and ongoing access to education. Their business is stronger and more profitable than others that don't put their people first. Strong teams keep the business running, even when the owner isn't around; they develop rich relationships with customers and their colleagues; and they live richer, more fulfilling personal lives. They feel great about their jobs and coming into work most days because they know:
- what their responsibilities and goals are
- how they contribute to the ongoing performance of the company
- they are well respected, and receive regular and clear communication about things that impact their work
- they are encouraged to provide feedback and ideas, and listened to when they do contribute
- they enjoy ongoing clarity regarding how they're measuring up against expectations
- they have a voice in important decisions in their areas of responsibility
- they'll share in the celebrations when their department or the company achieves key objectives and milestones

In this culture each member of the team will go the extra mile without being asked and help each other out, as well as hold each other accountable. They will give others the credit instead of hoarding it for themselves and will take responsibility when things go sideways. Jared Rothberger, a regional developer with Jan-Pro, prioritizes the environment his team works in: "I want a good environment for my employees. And we really put a lot of emphasis on that. And anything I can do to help my team, the franchise owners, we really try to not let those things [slip]. Again, it goes back to 'make it easy to be our customer.' But also, I want it easy to be an employee. I want it easy to be a franchise owner."

THE CUSTOMER

The customer who is greeted by exemplary service has their expectations met and even exceeded. This does not mean they always have a perfect experience, and if there is a shortfall it falls to the franchisee and their team to listen to the customer's concerns, figure out what went off course, and do what's necessary to make it right, all the while communicating back to the customer about resolution progress. The customer then knows that they are important. Just look at how Sean Hassan, a regional developer with Jan-Pro, applies this in an adverse situation:

> There's so many people who want to analyze a complaint and then get back to the customer or the person who made the complaint. And by then, it's been too long. So, I always train my people, especially my operations team, to acknowledge ASAP to the customer whether you have an answer or not. Keep people in the loop. Tell them, "This is what I'm discussing and my plan. This is what I'm going to do. This is when I'm going to get back to you." And then when you get back to the customer in the designated time frame, whether it's an hour or ten minutes, you say, "Okay, well, this is what I've found out since we last talked." And you keep communicating until there's resolution.

My takeaways from Sean's great example are to communicate right away with a customer and keep them aware of how their problem is being solved. People are generally reasonable and will understand that problems take time to solve. Just don't ever leave them in the dark. It's not just about solving problems, though. It's also about innovating and bringing new ideas, sometimes even before the client is aware of a need.

THE FRANCHISEE OWNER

Practicing servant leadership builds a culture of self-accountability and self-responsibility. The team has clarity around their roles and responsibilities, and receives constant feedback as to how their performance is stacking up against the goals. In this culture, the franchisee's financial and lifestyle goals have the strongest potential to be met and even exceeded. The owner can have peace of mind about the operation of the business because the team is well prepared, trained, and responsible, and will have each other's backs to collectively do what it takes to meet and exceed both the customer's and the franchise owner's expectations.

You have likely inferred that such a culture is a high-trust culture. And you'd be right. Sean Hassan talks about trusting his team to make the right decisions. And that means taking ownership, which he is happy to let them have. He says, "When my staff takes ownership for their roles and their responsibilities, and of course their actions and those roles and responsibilities and outcomes, then I put the limelight on them. We win together. When they win, I win."

Steve White inspires his team of franchisees by celebrating them and believing they can do greater things:

> We have got to take business to the next level, and the next level, and the next level. And the way you do that is by painting the vision for these franchise owners and by saying, "Okay, we're not going to diminish where you are. We're going to celebrate where you are. It's a good thing. It's a wonderful thing. But there's more beauty. There's

more greatness. There's more awesomeness out there to do. There's more good you can do for the world around you. And we're going to support you. Here's the next couple of steps on that path." And you have to keep them moving forward.

There's always more that you can do for your business and the world around you. And Steve's franchisees will accomplish these things because the leadership he models is authentic and humble and comes from the heart of a servant.

And finally, to me the absolute embodiment of servant leadership at the franchisee level is expressed in the wise words of Michael Gilpin, who cares so much about his team that he sees his employees as his most important relationships, even more so than his paying customers: "So, this one's more of my personal touch. I can list off my top sixteen customers by name, in the snap of a finger. And the reason is this—because my top sixteen customers are team members of FASTSIGNS of Grand Rapids, Michigan. My number one paying customer comes in at number seventeen."

Michael fully subscribes to the philosophy about treating your employees like your most important repeat customer.

THE FRANCHISOR

As you're likely beginning to see, franchisees who espouse and practice servant leadership are among the most satisfied and financially strong in the entire base of franchisees in the franchisor's system. As such, these unique franchisees drive value to the franchisor on multiple levels. The most obvious is generating consistently strong royalty revenues. Far more important though is the thought leadership and cultural contribution these servant leader franchisees make. As you'll see in chapter 7, they are among the biggest thought leadership contributors to driving operational excellence and are also typically the strongest validators when helping prospective franchisees assess the opportunity. All of these factors help to build brand awareness and also attract stronger future franchisees to the system.

While there will always be unhappy and underperforming franchisees (a topic of discussion in the next chapter), in a true servant leadership culture the mindset of next-level possibility thrives, and self-accountability and self-responsibility are core elements of that culture. There are plenty of franchisees who are running successful businesses and contributing to a healthy royalty stream for the franchisor. The servant leadership culture operates at an even higher level; it is one that creates a buzz, and that buzz will attract strong new franchisees and loyalty for the franchisee base.

Building Your Path to Servant Leadership

Let's look at several specific components of the path to developing a servant leadership philosophy, shared by my interviewees who have achieved astounding results with it.

INVEST IN YOURSELF

Shane Noble, a franchisee with Kitchen Tune-Up, was quick to point out that leading people requires an investment in yourself first. He told me,

> Learn to invest in yourself first, because I think that's the greatest investment you can make. It's multiplied fifty to a hundred times. It's your biggest investment over marketing or anything else—yourself. For me, before we get to a next level or whatever, I have to become it first, as myself, and then the business will follow.
>
> We have a team [of] about twenty-two of us right now. By the end of the year, we want to be a hundred-person team.
>
> I've invested in a leadership course, so that way I feel like if I can become that leader, then I'll attract that many more people and be able to lead that [much] bigger of a team. If I would have been my old self, that probably wouldn't happen. I think it's the same for everything, right? If you can't manage your personal finances, how could you ever plan on managing business financials? Because I think you're going to win by having the human capital, today.

Shane sees developing his leadership skillset as the key to growing his business, and that requires attracting people. He believes he has to prove his merits as a leader to make that happen, so he makes that investment. As a leader, where do see you see gaps in your professional development?

HIRE RIGHT

As a franchisee, the day-to-day operation of the business is your responsibility, and the responsibility of the team you build. It is safe to say that your hiring decisions are among the most important of any decisions in running your business. The reasons are:

- Your staff are executing on the brand's reputation and promise
- Your staff are on the frontline of interacting with your customers
- Your staff have to be adequately trained and be able to think on their feet
- Your staff have to have the internal motivation to want to provide exceptional customer service
- You want to retain your staff because good employees can move the business forward and reduce your costs from employee churn

The more that the visible face of your business to your customer relies on your team instead of you, the more valuable your business becomes as you build your business assets over time, which is important if selling your business is an exit strategy down the road.

Josh York, president and CEO of GYMGUYZ, told me his philosophy of hiring talent: "You need people to come on board who don't need to be motivated. They already have motivation. And the ones who succeed are the ones who are willing to learn and listen."

It is clear that self-motivation and a learning mindset are important in GYMGUYZ's hiring decisions. Why mindset is so important to Josh goes to the very heart of the theme of this book:

I constantly tell people that fear is a reaction. Courage is a choice. And I tell them all the time that to be in a business that's growing, like ours is, requires a resilient mindset. You have to have that resilient mindset, and the people who do have a growth mindset. There are two types of mindsets: fixed mindset and growth mindset. If you work with people with a fixed mindset, you'll never get to the next level.

Next-level growth is not possible with a fixed mindset and without having resilience. Josh links courage to resilience, meaning that taking action is rooted in these attributes.

As a leader, do you model a growth mindset? Do you see it in your people? Do the people you hire have the vision, drive and tenacity to achieve their dreams, regardless of the forces that work against them? As you learn how to hire and lead this kind of person, like will attract like. Your team will inspire one another.

INVEST IN THE TEAM

Franchisee Heather Stankard is the embodiment of a humble and genuine person. What she spoke to me about is a leadership essential:

> I always invest in my team. I have one employee who was there when I bought the franchise. Everyone else is new. I took my time building my business and building my staff, and definitely one of the biggest reasons that I'm successful is my team. I have open communication with them. I'm loyal to them. They're loyal to me. It's extremely important to me that they feel part of the team and that they feel valued, because without my employees I would not be where I am at all.

As a leader, how would you assess your level of communication with your team? How often do they tell you they feel valued? How often do you thank them for contributing to your success? Top Great Clips franchisee Clara Osterhage spoke about her team:

> So, I have an addiction, and my addiction is to these women who work in [our salons]. We're probably 96 percent female. Most of them are single head-of-household single parents. So the social

work side of me has this great place to live. I find myself in a place where them having great jobs, producing the most income that they can for themselves and for their families, is paramount for me. And I do [a] speech every year, and I share that every time. My addiction is to them. That's why we open more stores. It's not about having more stores. That's funny. But it's about adding more people. I am in a position to make a difference in their lives, and that's a big ding-dong deal for me.

How do your employees feel about being part of your team? Is your workplace culture closer to what Clara's team enjoys, or is it closer to the other end of the spectrum where they might be thinking of joining the quiet quitting movement?

COMMUNICATE CLEARLY AND OFTEN

Emily Wilcox, another successful Great Clips franchisee, spoke about engaging with employees and the importance of communication. She says,

> Developing your people is a critical aspect—making sure that they know what's expected of them. Don't assume that they know what something is. Help and guide them, so they know how to perform well in their role. So we spend a lot of time developing our stylists, our leaders. We're very actively involved in that from the day that somebody's hired. It's a critical piece of who we are.
>
> And, I think, communication. I mean, our employees hear from me… whether it's on Facebook or my voice on the phone. They're going to see me in the salons. I probably over-communicate, using as many avenues to communicate as possible. Knowledge is power, and the more that people know, the more that they're able to effectively do their job.

What I love about Emily's insights is that communication leads to knowledge, and knowledge is power. This is about empowering her people for life. It is another important message for leaders, which is that you influence your people beyond the business. By leading well, you equip your people with life skills. As for Emily's business, when her staff feel empowered, think of how that benefits the environment in her salons and customer retention and growth. Not to mention attracting new talent to her business.

Brad Rush had this to share about where and when to communicate:

> Care-frontation, yeah. You read [author Patrick] Lencioni—he talks about how no productive meetings take place without any conflict, and if everybody's always in agreement with everybody else, no one is pushing others to get better. So, I want people that are resolute enough and [know] what's important to them and understand what our overall objectives are, that when anybody deviates or gets off track, they're willing to broach the topic and have the conversation. And on the flip side of that, whoever is being addressed has to be receptive to listening to what they're being told with the understanding the only reason that conversation is taking place is because 1) that person talking to you cares about your success, and 2) they care about what we're trying to do as a group.

What gets communicated, and the frequency of that communication, are important considerations in three directions: franchisee to staff, staff to franchisee, and the one that's most often under-supported, staff to staff. In addition to communicating clear goals and expectations, the more that everyone knows what's going on and how their part to play fits in, the more effective the operation is going to be, which naturally drives better quality of work and higher results. Just look at what a few TPFs have to say about this.

Cynthia Keenan on transparency:

> I'm very transparent. I think communication is key. As much as I want this to be a happy, peaceful, and joyful environment, we are a business and our purpose as a business is to make money so that we can all pursue our own joys and happiness and have our own personal goals. So, I always approach it as, "This is our main objective. I will not be successful unless you're successful."

There's nothing more important to me than my employees' success, because if they're all doing what they need to be doing, then I will be successful. It just falls into line. So, my job in that is to make sure I communicate very clearly what my expectations are, and then hold people accountable.

Angela Brown on communicating activity progress:

Every single day we track [progress] on our wall on our boards. We have these indicators—your lead indicators—we have them all the time. I am big on customer satisfaction surveys, when certain stylists get shout-outs for doing a great job; that Net Promoter Score we get from our clients is a huge indicator for us. I will celebrate and reward the behaviors that are going to be instrumental to our success long-term—that's key. Another key is the selling of memberships: how often are you promoting membership sales within our bar. I celebrate and herald every staff member; I hate using that word "staff"—I use "team member." I have banned the word "employees" or "staff," because I want them to know [they] are an integral part of the team. Even our receptionist, she's a high school student that comes in part-time on weekends. That's why the team engagement piece is so important.

I really respect Angela's communication goals and measuring, and especially her take on communicating expectations: "I sit down with each team member and let them know their relative significance and importance, and how they contribute to the success of the team." Now that's worth repeating!

Bob Danielson, a top-performing franchisee with FASTSIGNS (before selling his business), on numbers and incentives:

You can't stay the same—either your sales are going to increase or they're going to decrease. It's very difficult to stay level. I like to provide incentives and bonuses, and those change over the years because I've found there's no top-of-mind awareness [of the goals and KPI dashboard without fresh incentives]. They lose that [awareness]. It's like, "Oh, great, we got an incentive." But there's no top-of-mind awareness. See, I have to keep that fresh. There's incentives and bonuses involved for everybody in the store.

Bob on empowering your people:

So right now, running the business, I depend on my store manager, sales manager and the inside sales, the whole crew, to take care of themselves. My manager sets daily and monthly goals for the salespeople. And then the actual numbers are put on our projection board, so everybody knows where they sit. And those numbers are updated weekly.

What I love about Bob's communication style is that he's empowered his manager to set the monthly targets, and that everybody has some form of incentive for their part of the picture, which is reviewed weekly. Wow—what a combination! It's no surprise that Bob was ranked in the top 25 of over 650 franchisees for over five years.

SHARE IDEAS

Edith Wiseman, president of FRANdata, gave me insights into sharing ideas and thinking outside the box that can attract people even in a tight labor market:

To me, an engaged franchisee is a growing franchisee. So what I mean by that is being engaged with the brand, and being engaged with what's going on, what's going to affect your business and your brand. So those who are absentee owners, and aren't really engaged in either way, I think over time there will be challenges to their business that they didn't see coming.

So, whether you're at a franchisee convention, or the IFA [International Franchise Association] convention, or are taking part in a franchisee forum, it's amazing how quickly you learn things that you can go back and implement in your business when you are in a group setting and discussing what your business challenges are.

I'm on the board this year of the IFA, and I always walk away from every meeting thinking, "Wow, these ten people just shared really incredible ideas as to how to deal with this ever-present problem that we have"—with labor, for instance. There's one guy who's going to create his own childcare. He's going to either buy a franchise in childcare, or he's going to create one himself, so that he can provide childcare to his employees. So it's about how to bring creativity to your problem solving, and I think engagement helps you infuse new ideas.

Edith touches on engagement here, and you'll see in the next chapter just how closely related engagement is to franchisee performance. Highly engaged franchisees significantly outperform less-engaged franchisees on a number of metrics.

EMPOWER YOUR TEAM

A final attribute of servant leadership I would like to comment on is empowerment. As a refresher, we have discussed investing in yourself to build your leadership capability; hiring the right people to lead; investing in your team; communicating often and with clarity; and making sure you share ideas with other franchisees and give new ideas a try. These attributes fall under the umbrella of empowerment. In my interview with Charles Bonfiglio, CEO of Tint World, he spoke about empowerment:

I think the top skillset for a leader, regardless of how qualified someone is in sales, operations, or the technical aspects, is being able to empower their employees to do a good job and own their position. The franchisee can work on the business and not need to be in it every day, because they're empowering leaders within their business system, and that allows them to grow more units with more staff who take care of the customer in the same way as if they were there, but by being a leader.

Empowerment is having a program where people want to work for them—where the people like the franchisee, trust the franchisee, and feel there's a future with that person. That's the leadership ability top performers have. Those are the ones that have sustainable businesses and are growing. No matter what, that's a key quality. Otherwise, you're always going to have turbulence, because you're not empowering the right people with the right mindset. You have to have a good culture.

Charles says that successful businesses are built on relationships, and delegating responsibility requires trust. Think for a moment about how putting trust in your people will make them feel. Much like Edith's focus on engagement, putting trust in someone will lift them up. And they just might lift the business too.

Next-level growth is a result of having a team with a growth mindset, led by strong leadership, that has loyalty to the brand, fellow employees, and your customers. Next-level growth is also achieved by understanding that communication equals knowledge which equals power. Finally, no matter what, trust is a key quality.

GROWTH PLAN EXERCISE 5-1
Periodically Revisiting the Key Questions

At the beginning of the chapter I asked you to think about describing your leadership style according to three questions; this is something you should do at least once annually. Please complete the survey below, and then think about those three questions again. How might your original answers be different?

- How effectively are you creating opportunities for your people to excel and grow?
- In what ways are you setting them up for success by building the right environment?
- How often do you acknowledge their contributions as meaningful in moving the business forward?

SURVEY 5-1:

How Prepared Am I to Lead a Business that Will Attract and Keep the Best and Brightest?

Respond to the statements below on a scale of 1 (rarely) to 5 (always).	1	2	3	4	5
1. I model the attributes and behaviors that I want to see in my people.					
2. I genuinely care about my people and have regard for their success, safety and security.					
3. A high degree of communication is expected among the team and between leader and team.					
4. I remind my team all the time that challenges have to be met with an open mind and that old solutions may not work for new types of problems.					
5. I can comfortably tell my team and peers I am not the smartest person in the room.					
6. I encourage my team to bring ideas to the table.					
7. I believe that learning is the key to having a leadership mindset.					
8. I allow room for failure when the intent is honest and the effort is real.					
9. I develop leadership skills in my people and build my own leadership skills in kind.					
10. I believe that a growth mindset will open doors for advancement for my team.					
11. I believe that a growth mindset enables critical thinking and problem solving.					
12. I invest in my own leadership growth.					

Respond to the statements below on a scale of 1 (rarely) to 5 (always).	1	2	3	4	5
13. My team has seen me take on menial tasks, such as sweeping the floor.					
14. I regularly give my team stretch assignments that allow them to test their capabilities.					
15. I believe that mistakes are opportunities for teaching moments.					
16. I ask for feedback from my team on my leadership style.					
17. I believe that trust leads to loyalty, which is essential for retaining staff.					
18. I am committed to working on the business every day and growing it through developing my people.					
19. We strive to serve one another and our customers from the heart as well as the mind.					
20. We regularly remind ourselves of our mission to do better every day.					

What do your responses tell you about where improvements need to be made? Consider sharing the survey with your employees. If any might be nervous about taking the survey, make it a blind one. Then you can get a true measure of your leadership practice and how well you are growing your people.

TO CLOSE THIS CHAPTER, here are insights from Colin Bates on a core leadership skill, which is to always ask what can be done better:

I constantly challenge my people to build scalable, sustainable processes. I will say, "We're going to grow this business. In everything that you do in a day, ask yourself, 'Is this the most efficient and effective way? Or are we doing it this way because it fits our needs today, as opposed to looking at what we need to do in the future?'" Sometimes it's difficult for people to break old ways of thinking.

We need to be thinking about not so much where we are, but where we're going. How are we going to get there? What are we going to do when we get there?

In the next chapter we discuss what it takes to master the system. What does it take? Discipline, passion, commitment, risk tolerance, street smarts—maybe all of the above? If there is a repeatable and successful formula, why aren't all franchisees performing at an optimal level? Well, you are about to find out.

Driver No. 4 Takeaways

List your top three takeaways from this chapter:

1. _____
2. _____
3. _____

CHAPTER 6

DRIVER NO. 5
Master the System

I'VE SELECTED TWO QUOTES to open this chapter; please take a moment to reflect on them. The first is from Ned Lyerly, who discusses the top-performing franchisees in the CKE (Hardee's and Carl's Jr.) family:

> The franchisees who perform at the highest level are franchisees that are very purposeful about what they do. They're one hundred percent committed to their business and their people. And they have a level of passion and commitment to what they're doing and work at connecting to everyone in their business to make it successful.
>
> I think it's really a special quality of top franchisees, particularly those that have been in systems for a while, that they're so passionate about the brand. And then so passionate about doing things right.

And now let's hear from Clara Osterhage, a Great Clips multi-unit franchisee, who speaks about culture and values:

> We nailed our values and have not modified them since we wrote them up four years ago. The first one is, "We are passionate about

the brand." The second one is, "We are kind." The third one is, "We do whatever it takes." The fourth one is, "We do what we say." The fifth one is, "We have integrity." And the last one is, "We have fun."

What stands out for me is that Clara and Ned speak about shared values, a deep connection and commitment to the brand, and representing the brand with purpose, passion and integrity.

And values are fine to express, but it is another thing entirely to implement them. Ned talks about doing things right, and Clara talks about doing whatever it takes. Every franchisee has to go through a learning journey fraught with challenges, adversity, pain, and excitement—and a good mix of wins and losses. In other words, they have to *do*. They have to learn, make mistakes, grow, and evolve into a successful business owner. Much of that learning is focused on understanding a system and its operational drivers. For that to happen, it is incumbent on franchisees to draw upon the knowledge and experience of their franchisor's leadership team and other successful franchisees within their system.

Those I interviewed attributed low or unsatisfactory performance to a fundamental failure to follow the system. So the message is crystal clear: if you want to achieve success in franchise ownership, then learn the system and follow it.

To follow the system, though, the franchisee has to accept that they are a student, wet behind the ears, even if they made their way to the C-suite before turning to franchising. What they believe about the way a business should be run might not be applicable to the franchise system they bought into. The wisdom given by interviewees and shared with you here is: "Learn the system and then, over time, master the system. Once the basics are mastered, then optimize the business in collaboration with the franchisor."

Optimizing their business is where TPFs live and thrive. Mastery is never "done." And TPFs exist in every franchise system that has proven to be a viable business model. Becoming a TPF is an achievable goal for any franchisee willing to employ the right combination of mindset, determination, focus, and patience. And TPFs achieve that level by treating that path as a learning journey.

Let's dive deep into that journey. As we do, assess what phase you're currently in. It might surprise you that franchisee tenure is not linked to ongoing progress and growth.

The Franchisee's Growth Journey

This growth journey is a path every franchisee will travel. Like any well-traveled path, there are many detours, exit points, and points of re-entry. Sometimes franchisees are not even aware that they have left the path until they feel the sting of nettles and brambles. What I mean is that franchisees who lose their focus end up being stuck working *in* the business instead of leading their team and working *on* their business, or fail to follow their franchisor's system and put their business in jeopardy.

A cause of struggle is lack of belief in, or alignment with, the system. You might say, "Gary, why does this happen? You invest in a proven model so why not follow it to a T?" That is a million-dollar question. In my interview with Joel Winters, he spoke passionately about this. You'll recall this quote excerpted in chapter 3, and it's worth repeating here:

> Oh man, I can't overemphasize the value of [following the system]. Look, if you're buying a franchise and you're not leveraging that, or the franchisor is not helping you leverage it or making it available, it's a real missed opportunity. For instance, we've been in business two and a half years, but there are certain other locations that have been in business for thirty years, just like Kitchen Tune-Up [the franchisor], and that experience is utterly inaccessible to most business owners. To not avail yourself of it is ludicrous. We really believe in that, and it's been instrumental in our success... [We] could never overestimate the importance of that.

Let's first understand that the franchisee's learning journey is a balancing act of time, focus, money, and energy, and this holds true for the entire life cycle of the ownership journey. How the franchisee embraces this journey will largely determine their over-all performance outcomes.

THE THREE PHASES OF THE GROWTH JOURNEY

There are three distinct phases of the franchisee growth journey:

Phase 1: Learning the system

Phase 2: Knowing the system

Phase 3: Mastering the system

In Part Two of this book I introduce the Growth Helix and the six steps the franchisee can take to continuously and incrementally build a better business. (As you work through the Growth Helix, you will create a playbook for your business.) Each growth journey phase is comprised of a series of growth cycles, sometimes strung back to back and sometimes layered one on top of another. Think of it this way: as the franchisee achieves proficiency in one skill area, they expand their scope of abilities and become ready to progress to the next area.

The objective of progressing through the three growth phases is achieving operational excellence. Progress is driven by a) the current and emerging priorities of your business, and b) working on and mastering each of the core proficiencies of your franchisor's sub-systems (see chapter 3). If you sense you are somehow just standing still, that is a strong signal of a danger point. Be resilient and heed the advice of TPFs to not underestimate how deep and long your learning curve can be.

PHASE 1: LEARNING THE SYSTEM: START BUILDING
THE FOUNDATION

Duration: From launch to about twenty-four months, depending on variables such as the complexity of the franchise system, the quality of the franchisor's onboarding process and support/coaching meth-odologies, and the learning capabilities of the franchisee.

This is the first phase that every new franchisee goes through, and the one that is most under-anticipated by prospective franchisees. Once the franchise has been purchased, a whirlwind of activity begins. The franchisee is drinking in knowledge from multiple fire-hoses. Not only does the franchisee have to learn the on-the-job skills of the various positions of future employees, they also have to learn the back-office skills of strategic planning, marketing, tracking and data analysis, financial management, and human resources. Whether a new build or an existing location, in both cases design, equipment, and protocols come into play.

The franchisee has to take in information at a blistering pace and constantly think about what they're doing and how to do it. The franchisor provides help both directly and indirectly (initial onboarding training, and ongoing coaching and support). Some tasks are simple and repetitive; some activities are more complex and require close attention and practice.

Sometimes part of the learning process is to unlearn previous ways of doing things. The new franchisee is highly dependent on their franchisor at this stage to guide and focus their effort. The franchisor expects that the new franchisee will follow the instructions and learn to execute the system as prescribed—after all, isn't access to that system one of the primary reasons why they bought the franchise?

....

Put your creativity on the shelf for the first two years. That's not to completely stifle it. When you have ideas, capture and journal them for the future, but first learn the how and why of what the franchisor is teaching you, which might take several months of hard work to completely see the nuances of a successful business model.

....

Jason Zickerman points out:

People don't come to The Alternative Board to buy a job. They come here because it is a passion and whatnot. But at the same time, for these people it's been a long time since they were not good at something. And so that skillset to learn something new, to commit to becoming excellent, and to be willing to make mistakes that you haven't made maybe for years and from an earlier career, and be forgiving to a certain point, but committed to becoming better, is mission critical. So developing that skillset, the new skills needed and that commitment to it, and that desire to have excellence in how they execute, is huge.

It's quite common for new franchisees to be compliant and follow the system in certain areas, while resisting complying in other areas; often this resistance stems from prior career success, from a different way of doing things. But that was in an entirely different work environment. Being able to pick and choose what parts of the franchise system to use, and which to ignore, is counterintuitive and counterproductive. Remember, you bought the franchise to realize an accelerated path to success, and that path comes with learning different ways of doing things, even if you don't agree with them or don't like them.

Unlike starting a business from scratch or buying an existing business, as a franchisee you can't just say things like "I don't like that so I'm not going to do it" or "That doesn't work for me, so I'm going to keep doing things the way I've done in my previous job." The franchisor has an expectation that every new franchisee will actively seek to learn the brand's processes and systems as they onboard, because that's what it takes to deliver on the brand's promise. The franchisor also has an expectation that existing franchisees learn and adopt new systems as they're introduced over time. By signing your franchise agreement and paying your franchise fee, you've committed to learning new skillsets.

Franchisors have heard thousands of justifications for *not* following the system in this first phase. Every one of them is an excuse, and a defense mechanism of the new franchisee for sticking to what's comfortable. Well, buying a franchise and running a business is an exercise in discomfort, so the sooner one realizes this, the sooner they can stop working against themselves. Josh Skolnick reminded me of this when we spoke:

Keep in mind that every franchise candidate tells you "I'm going to be accountable. I'm going to do the right thing. I'm going to get up and I'm going to work hard to build my business" when you're in the development process. And we tell everybody, "Starting a new business, if you make the commitment to work harder than you've ever worked in your life for the next twenty-four months, put more into this in the next twenty-four months than anything you've ever done in your life, you're going to get yourself to a place where the return on investment and return on time will be second to none."

And everybody's willing to do that up-front, but actions speak louder than words. And then you'd be surprised, once they get in, there's always an excuse, something in the way of why they didn't do it. I always call the excuses the should haves, could haves, would haves—*we should have invested in this, we would have invested in this, or we could have invested in this*—but there's always objections as to why we didn't.

It's hard to actually put everything into action. And so, when somebody does take all those proper steps, it really sets them up for success.

As I've mentioned, a big part of progressing though this first and foundation-building stage is to let go of old ways and to accept and begin applying the accumulated knowledge of the collective brain trust, which includes the franchisor and all of the franchisees who have joined the system before you. Like Josh says, the system can set you up for success. Dan Monaghan, founder of Clear Summit Group, would agree:

Another area that is important that we saw in the data is that skepticism of top performers was lower than under-performers'. People who are constantly second-guessing a system might be better not to be franchisees. There is a huge amount of time and money you have to put in. When you buy a franchise, you're standing on the shoulders of giants who came before you. And there is room for innovation and constant enhancement, and part of that depends on the system. But if you don't understand that you're already working with a proven system, and you're trying to second-guess that constantly, and you're second-guessing what the franchisor is telling you, you're going to get suboptimal results.

If you choose to ignore or reject too many components of the system, then you might never evolve out of the learning phase, regardless of how many years you own your franchise. The bottom quartile of the franchisee performance bell curve is disproportionately populated with franchisees that resist or outright fight against doing things as recommended by the franchisor.

HOW TO OPTIMIZE RESULTS IN PHASE 1

Create a study plan with the help of your franchisor. (This is a great idea throughout the running of your franchise.) This is not an operational growth plan; rather, it is intended to actively review, on at least a monthly basis, the foundation of your business and check for cracks. Then you have to figure out what is required to fix those cracks. The questions that can guide this plan are as follows:

- What are the primary roles I need to execute to get the business launched and established?
- What support systems do I need to become intimately familiar with (e.g., CRM, KPI dashboard)? (It never ceases to amaze me how so many franchisees use only a fraction of the franchisor's systems, which provide market intelligence and customer and operational data. Also see chapter 4.)
- What are my biggest skill gaps (weaknesses) that I can/must hire for?
- What knowledge resources are available to me and my team (e.g., training and operations manuals, videos, articles and case studies available on the franchisor's intranet; coaching sessions with head office support; peer franchisee mentorship)?
- How well have I set clear knowledge growth goals with timelines? How well do I understand how to measure proficiency improvement

among my team at set milestones? How can my franchisor provide guidance to improve here?
- How well do I engage my learning coach (usually a field support coach from the franchisor's leadership team) and book frequent learning sessions at regular intervals?
- Have my franchisor and I scheduled progress review sessions?

Build on your strengths. Recall these points from the awareness exercise in chapter 4:
- Identify your top skills
- Identify gaps between the way you know how to do things and the way your franchisor needs things done
- Identify what new skills need to be developed (where you have limited prior experience or knowledge)
- Build a learning plan to close those gaps

Building on your strengths requires being intentional and focused. Angela Brown explains, "You have to be intentional on how you approach your business every day. For me, there are challenges every single day, but it just becomes a part of our capital, which means you are only as valuable as your problem-solving skills. The more challenges we take on and can overcome, the more valuable we become. The more we're able to take on, the more we grow bigger."

As you add key staff and grow your business, you'll want to build this learning plan with each staff member so that you can help them grow, while also getting solid practice in one of the critical skills of running most businesses—leadership.

Starting with your first hires, if you communicate expectations, provide learning support and direction, and set the expectation of self-accountability and self-responsibility, you'll be building the kind of culture where people look forward to coming to work, and they'll go the extra mile to exceed your and your customers' expectations. Don't wait until you're two years into running your business to begin this type of training of your staff. By then it will be too late and bad habits will have already become entrenched.

....

Something to be mindful of for new franchisees here is that, from day one, either you're starting to build the kind of culture that will give your team the opportunity to thrive and your customers to love, or you're building a less appealing culture, accidentally. How you show up yourself; how you hire, train, coach, and support your people; and how you interact with customers and deliver on your commitments are visible to all. Remember the old saying "Speed of the leader, speed of the pack." If you're critical and negative about the system, consider the message you are sending to the team. Just like you, they may think it's okay to bend *your* rules. How does *that* make you feel?

....

PHASE 1 CLOSING THOUGHTS

A key part of the learning strategy is to prioritize the order of learning. The objective in Phase 1 is to get to a point of proficiency and lay the foundation to progress to mastery. The time it takes to advance your skills from brand-new to proficient is significant. Focus on the core skills required to execute the franchisor's business systems and processes.

Adam Contos is a big fan of aiming for consistency: "Like working out, [top-performing franchisees] do the work to create results consistently and relentlessly. You know, I use the phrase 'no one can do your push-ups for you' a lot. Consistency builds productive habits. And that's ultimately what we're trying to do with a franchise. We're trying to take a framework of demonstrated success and create productive habits out of that in order to replicate that success."

When you're consistently producing good results in a number of the KPIs in your franchisor's dashboard, then you're likely in the process of evolving into Phase 2: Knowing the System.

PHASE 2: KNOWING THE SYSTEM: MOVING FROM PROFICIENCY TO MASTERY

Duration: Minimum two to three years from start of Year 3. Reduced and even minimal dependence on the franchisor.

The second phase is about operating from a place of some accumulated and internalized knowledge, while recognizing that there's still a lot of learning in store and much growing yet to be done. A key indicator that a franchisee has moved into the Knowing the System phase is that they no longer have to think about how to execute on certain aspects of the business.

As the franchisee progresses through the second phase, they invest more time in learning about what aspects of the business deliver the highest return, and what drivers will scale the business. The franchisee knows the essentials of the "how"; now the focus is on how to get consistently better at the business and move from proficiency to mastery in each key driver area. The franchisee must lead the team with the same objective in mind—to help each team member get consistently better at performing their core duties and responsibilities. As Adam Contos said, the attitude for success is to be consistent and relentless.

As the franchisee and their team gets to a place of practiced proficiency in some areas, they'll want to then shift their focus to the next subsystem and use the learning plan strategy to help narrow the focus and drive deeper understanding and proficiency. Some team members will require refreshers, but that is to be expected.

In order to progress, heed the words of Dave Mortensen: "Everyone has their unique skills, but the ones that are really good at running a great system understand the operations and the basics of those operations and execute them at a high level, similar to any good athlete that you watch."

With a focus on continuous improvement, the franchisee will come to the realization that the initial training, coaching, and support they received from the franchisor to get to this point (during the learning phase) isn't enough to keep them on their growth trajectory. They are shifting from dependence on the franchisor to independence. The franchisee has learned enough to operate fairly independently of the franchisor's support. While adhering to the franchisor's system, the franchisee is responsible and accountable for results.

David Druker, president of The UPS Store, Canada, uses a training wheels metaphor for franchisees in the second phase:

> When you get to a certain level, you [say]: "I think I can guide myself. I think that maybe I could take the training wheels off." But those aren't training wheels. If you were to compare it to top athletes, they don't say, "I'm a top athlete now. I can stop training. I can go and eat chocolate cake and I don't have to worry about going to the gym. And I don't have to hone my skills." To stay at the top of your game, regardless of what your game is—if you're a doctor, a franchisee or if you're a hockey player, you've got to keep getting your skills better.

Testing a few boundaries and experimenting around the edges is risky if done too early in this phase because the franchisee has likely not mastered enough of the core components of the model. Do staff need more training? Are customers returning? Are there small successes to be celebrated? People, time and money resources that would be better used to continue refining things get squandered on experiments that the franchisee might not be ready for, or ready to learn from.

Let's be clear: experimenting is an important part of this second phase, but it should happen later on in the phase, after the franchisee and their team are performing the core roles and producing results consistently at or above desired levels. So how does one know when they're ready to start experimenting around the edges of the franchisor's model? The answer is in the data.

Data the business takes in must be measurable and able to be communicated in a way the team can understand it. This is the way data are impactful. Key Performance Indicators are designed to use data to help businesses understand how healthy they are. KPIs aggregate data that are tracked, measured and communicated. Essential KPIs are sales, revenue and costs, for example. The franchisor will introduce KPIs to the franchisee in the learning phase, but the benefit to the business requires application on a consistent basis.

Franchisees who make tracking and communicating KPI data one of their core learning objectives in the Knowing the System phase will find that they have far more confidence in themselves and their team. They will make better decisions and enjoy significantly higher levels of success than those franchisees that don't learn this skill. What do KPIs mean to a business? Dave Mortensen says that a veteran would tell a new franchisee to "know your numbers. Have a financial fluency in the business."

Cynthia Keenan would agree. She says, "Don't be afraid of your numbers. Look at them monthly. Some people look daily. Some numbers I was definitely checking daily, and made sure they were going up. Make sure they're on the trend that you want them to be. It's an analysis tool. Do not spend time on goals that are not driving the business forward."

It's amazing how many franchisees have an inadequate grasp of their numbers. In contrast, TPFs are astute with their numbers, because numbers factor into every part of the business. They're going to know their lead measures, and they're going to know their lagging measures. (Utilizing KPIs is so important that chapter 8 is dedicated to this subject.)

THE FORK IN THE INDEPENDENCE ROAD

At some point in Phase 2, the franchisee comes to a fork in the road: Path A is the route where they can choose to operate mostly independently, having to a large degree achieved the financial and lifestyle goals they set. They have a good amount of operating freedom and are interacting minimally with their franchisor and peer franchisees. They are on a fairly flat growth trajectory, but that's okay because they are comfortable enough.

Path B is a tougher route to travel. Similar to Path A, the franchisee is doing relatively well at achieving their financial and lifestyle goals, but staying where they are isn't good enough. They want to take some part of their business to the next level. They recognize they don't have all of the answers, and understand that if they can tap into the collective brain trust of their franchise system, the pace of learning, growth, and results can be substantially accelerated. But to get there, they must ask for help—and they do ask.

For the franchisees that choose this more challenging second path, they see engaging with the collective brain trust as one of the keys to mastering their business systems and growing their leadership skills. It is while in the second phase that the franchisee must become more aware of what's going on across the entire franchise system. Which franchisees are innovating, and where and how? What's working well that can be leveraged in their own business? What mistakes have others made that can and should be avoided?

It's about leveraging the knowledge and experience of the lessons learned from their peer franchisees. It's also about beginning to be a contributor to and influencer for the collective brain trust by sharing their own lessons learned from both wins and losses.

LEVERAGING THE COLLECTIVE BRAIN TRUST

Think for a moment about the collective brain trust, which is the sum of all the knowledge and experience of every executive and support person at the franchisor's head office, and likewise of all the franchisees in the system who are willing to share their experiences for the betterment of all. Dan Monaghan equates it to power:

> In the world of franchising, the power comes from everyone sharing. Because that gives us competitive advantage if we're moving faster than our competitors and if we're learning faster than our competitors. And so, a new idea could emerge anywhere within the system. What that means is you're going to constantly be getting new ideas, and the system's going to constantly be evolving. But you also have to be a contributor to that. And everyone has different strengths and weaknesses, and in the things they bring to the table. But being willing to share is an important success trait.

Here are some questions to ask to help you identify resources when building your growth plan:

- Which franchisees in my system have mastered the skills I need to get to my next level? What are they doing that I'm not, and what are they doing better or more efficiently than me?

- Which franchisees with market characteristics similar to mine are maximizing their markets in ways that I'm not?

- Which franchisees have built excellent teams, where my key staff could learn from their key staff?

- What are the best practices that have bubbled up from the franchisee network that I've not yet implemented?

The franchisees that elect to travel along Path B become progressively more aware of the power of the franchisor's brand and system. As they travel farther down this path, they internalize the symbiotic aspect of their relationships with their franchisor and peer franchisees. And in doing so, they also start giving back to the system; instead of just drawing on the knowledge base of the collective brain trust like they do in Phase 1 and early in Phase 2, they start adding to it by sharing their own best practices with the franchisor and peer franchisees, participating in committees and leading conference sessions.

An important side note here is that franchisees who choose this second path are constantly seeing value from being part of their franchise system and generally feel they're getting a relatively equitable exchange of value for their royalty dollar. Franchisees who choose the first path, however—those that remain more independent and who don't utilize many of the knowledge resources of the franchisor and their peer franchisees—typically demonstrate a pattern of diminishing satisfaction with their franchisor over time. They get to a point where they're constantly asking, "What have you done for me lately?" They lack faith in the system. Mary Thompson puts it this way:

If they would just try the system. They are always trying to either reinvent the system or tell you that some part of the system doesn't work, or doesn't work for them, or doesn't work in their market. Or they will say, "You're not here on your feet or on the street doing this—you don't understand." And it comes back to almost a faith. They'll say, "Show me the numbers or the data, or show me..." And it's like, first of all, you bought this franchise based on everything we did already show you. Secondly, we have literally hundreds and hundreds [of franchisees] that are doing it and doing it well. Now you've got to have the faith to actually go do it.

And then to me, it's [taking] the system and the action hand-in-hand. Some of them will say, "I believe in the system," but they don't take any action. And others are taking action, but it's actions *away* from the system. But usually they have a lack of faith and they express it... They'll say things like, "Well, yeah, I know that I'm supposed to do the fourteen steps in approaching the customer, but..." And as soon as they say "but," I know as a business coach they don't believe in what they've been taught.

It's no surprise that franchisees on Path A are some of the least happy franchisees in the system. They struggle too long and too hard with certain parts of their business. They keep their heads down and make the same mistakes over and over again, and thus they are stuck and stay stuck. They commiserate with other Path A franchisees about all that's wrong with the franchise system.

Path A is a side loop path, as the franchisee's journey on this path occasionally loops back and intersects again with that fork in the road they faced earlier in their growth journey—either remain mostly independent and somewhat less happy, or admit there might be a better way. Some franchisees see the light of the second path and realize that Path A has been a detour, and that in order to get the most out of their business and out of the relationship with their franchisor, they have to switch paths, and get onto Path B.

What's great about this is that, regardless of a franchisee's tenure with their franchise, once they choose to embrace the learning journey more fully and intentionally, they can radically improve the results of their business in a relatively short period of time. This is a key message that Colin Bates promotes. Colin says, "With Jan-Pro, you have the ability to work within the framework that's provided to you to make your franchise better. I would encourage [franchise owners] to look at what they bring to the table that could make the business better. If that's not your core strength, then listen to others that have done that. Don't be afraid to try it in your own organization."

There are countless stagnation-to-high-performance stories within the franchise industry—a tenured franchisee's performance is flat for several years, then seemingly all of a sudden their trajectory skyrockets and they achieve amazing, sustained results. This is what can happen when a franchisee switches from Path A to Path B.

In taking Path B, the franchisee is engaged by and builds a vibrant culture. Path B is characterized by energy, drive, and seemingly endless possibility. The leadership dimension we've spoken at length about also emerges. Path A, however, leads to complacency and diminished returns. Path A cultures, once set, are far more difficult to grow out of, so reflect deeply on which path you've chosen to be on. If you're on Path A, seek that fork in the road where you can merge back onto Path B. If you do not actively look to find Path B, improved results will continue to be elusive.

HOW TO OPTIMIZE RESULTS IN PHASE 2

Here are some questions to guide your thinking on Phase 2 growth:
- What are the primary roles I need to master to take my business to the next level?
- What roles have I mastered (operating at a proficiency I've rated at 8.5 out of 10 or better)?
- Which of my team members can I train to take on more responsibility and by doing so free up my time to focus on highest-return activities? (Note: Be specific as to matching responsibilities to the individual.)

- What support systems have I and team members mastered?
- What additional support systems do I need to study to become proficient with the tools available to me (e.g., KPI dashboards, P&Ls, financial statements)?
- What skill gaps (weaknesses) do I need to hire for?
- What new knowledge resources are available to my team and me (conferences, franchisee peer group meetings, boot camps, shared best practices, peer franchisee mentors, course offerings from institutions like financial management for non-financial managers, etc.)?
- Have I set personal knowledge growth goals with timelines to assess proficiency improvements, for myself as well as key staff members?
- Do I engage my learning coach (usually a field support coach from the franchisor's leadership team) frequently enough?
- Do I hold progress reviews with my team frequently enough?

As I previously mentioned, this phase of the learning journey is far more self-driven. Franchisees have to become intentional about making time for their personal growth and the growth of their team, because as the business grows, new choke points emerge. It's easy to get so caught up in the week-to-week work stuff that making time for growth gets put aside.

PHASE 2 CLOSING THOUGHTS

Most franchisees, by a wide margin, remain in Phase 2 for the duration of their tenure in their business. They could be stuck or simply complacent, lacking the internal drive to diagnose the problem and fix it. Other franchisees have a good level of business and a lifestyle they are enjoying, so progressing to the next level is a nice-to-have, but not a need-to-have. They see no need to exert the energy and deploy the resources required to grow further. But that too is complacency, and top performers do not live there. Ken LeBlanc, CEO of Property Guys, is clear on this point: "To give our franchisees a cookie-cutter way of operating and being successful is almost impossible, but we tell them that coming in. So, we look for people who are what we call 'structured entrepreneurs.' These people are going to follow the system but know full well they need to make that system their own in the market. That would probably be the one thing that jumps out most as far as [identifying consistent and top performers]. It's very, very big."

PHASE 3: MASTERING THE SYSTEM

Mastering the system is the ultimate destination of the learning journey; it is where TPFs live and breathe. But this does not mean that the journey is at an end. Instead, the learning journey evolves to mastering operational excellence, while also driving scalability. In order to achieve next-level growth, new market opportunities have to be identified and pursued; new choke points emerge and have to be resolved; and TPFs focus on attacking those opportunities and choke points with discipline, progressively building skills so that they can adjust more quickly.

Jason Zickerman maintains there is a status attached to being a top performer: "Top performers want to be acknowledged as top performers. Top performers want to be put in the position where they are with other top performers. Being part of that club. There's something about grit; excellence likes to be around excellence. But they want to be in that group of excellence not because they want the label of the club, but because they are excited by the idea that they could learn from other people who are excellent." Not all franchisees that operate in the third phase are top performers. TPFs are an elite group.

However, franchisees in this phase do understand this is where the team is fully built and highly trained. They have an unwavering focus on clearly stated objectives, and understand KPIs. Resilience is an important cultural value. The team knows that there are external forces at play that cause good and bad things to happen; their mindset is, "Okay, what are we going to do about it? How can we make the most of it?" Mastery is not "one-and-done"; in order to keep the momentum and retain a state of mastery, the franchisee and their team must perform in a constant state of self-accountability and self-responsibility. Jared Rothberger talks about a culture where people take ownership for the good and the bad:

> If you point at somebody else, if they screwed up, there's probably something you could have done better in that situation. When we have our staff meetings, we don't say, "Well, this person screwed this up," because everybody would point at them and talk about what that person did that was wrong. Rather, we open a conversation: "In this situation, what could we do better?" And usually, the person who screwed up is going to be the first one to say, "Here's what I didn't do. And here's what I'm going to do next time."
>
> And it's just that culture of ownership. But you can't have that culture of ownership without being able to forgive and be understanding.
>
> So it goes both ways. The person who it's costing financially [the business owner] needs to be in the mindset of, "This is training my staff. These are expenses that are training my staff and teaching them lessons on professional development. It is not a waste of money."

And importantly, it's not just about the franchisee and their business. Interdependence is the predominant aspect of the relationship between the franchisee and their franchisor, as well as between the franchisee and their peer franchisees. The interdependent franchisee is passionate about their brand, and about representing their brand in their community. They see themselves as part of the brand and see the brand as an integral part of their business.

HOW TO OPTIMIZE RESULTS IN PHASE 3

Here are some questions to guide your thinking on progressing through Phase 3:

- What level of maturity has my relationship with my franchisor progressed to?
- Am I able to find the answers to questions that relate to how my business has become more complex?

- How well have I prepared my team to work optimally?
- Are my peers and I regularly sharing information and ideas?
- Is our delivery of customer experience uniform and of the highest quality?
- How must my leadership attributes continue to evolve to reach a level of mastery?

PHASE 3 CLOSING THOUGHTS

Franchisees in the third phase of learning growth are the beacons of performance and excellence that newer franchisees seek to emulate; they are the thought leaders of the franchise system. They are highly active and involved, both in their own businesses and in finding ways to strengthen the brand and system. These are the people you'll see on the franchise advisory councils and special project committees; sometimes they even have a seat on the franchisor's board of directors. They have earned a place at the franchisor's strategy table because they have evolved to a point where they see the greatest path to success is to put the franchise system's interests ahead of their own. Their mindset is "Together, we win more"—more market share, more operating margin, more happiness and satisfaction, and all of it more frequently.

TPFs exist and thrive in an ongoing state of interdependence with their franchisor, with the body of franchisees within their system, and with their own business communities. The state of interdependence is the focus of the next chapter. Before you turn the page, however, take the time to complete the survey.

SURVEY 6-1:
Your Learning Phase Status

Use this survey to assess your status with respect to the three learning phases.

On a scale of 1 to 3, rate yourself on the following questions.	1 Some-times	2 Often	3 Always
PHASE 1: Learning the System. If my business is at this level:			
1. I take the time to continue to build on the foundation of the business by working on the system.			
2. I go by the book and have no desire to go outside the franchisor's system.			
3. I work continuously with my field coach to improve our system proficiency.			
4. My team and I have no trouble taking in and applying any modifications the franchisor makes to the system.			
5. I understand that I am learning a new skillset and may have to put aside methods that have given me past business success.			
6. I have a positive attitude that sustains my confidence in progressing to higher levels of system management.			
7. I work to a learning plan that has milestones.			
8. I ensure my employees have the tools, time, and other resources to learn their roles well.			
PHASE 2: Knowing the System. If my business is at this level:			
1. I am confident we have the core process locked down tight.			
2. I understand the team looks to me for leadership to continue to grow our proficiency and our business.			
3. I understand the KPIs we need to focus on to solve any problems and grow the business.			
4. I understand the competitive advantage of being aware of our brand, system-wide.			

On a scale of 1 to 3, rate yourself on the following questions.	1 Some-times	2 Often	3 Always
5. I stay informed of best practices that emerge from other franchisees.			
6. I provide meaningful feedback to my team on their progress.			
PHASE 3: Mastering the System. If my business is at this level:			
1. My team and I have grown our customer base.			
2. My team and I use a suite of KPIs that provide us with the right data we need for growth.			
3. I understand that professional development for my staff is not a hardship but a necessary expense that has measurable return on investment.			
4. My team and I are excited to be brand ambassadors in our community.			
5. I have earned the right to be at my franchisor's strategy table.			
6. My team and I celebrate achieving our milestones, without fail.			

YOUR SCORE: If you pencilled in any 1's or 2's, that is a sign of where you need to devote focus and energy to close the gaps. In your Growth Plan Workbook, write down ideas and action steps you can take both on your own and with your team to drive mastery.

Driver No. 5 Takeaways

List your top three takeaways from this chapter:

1. _____

2. _____

3. _____

CHAPTER 7

DRIVER NO. 6
Grow Your Interdependence

THE EVIDENCE OF THE LINK between high performance in franchise ownership and interdependence with the franchisor is undeniable. *Every* top performer I interviewed had evolved their relationship with the franchisor to a highly interdependent one. This chapter will help you identify where you are on the franchisee maturity spectrum and what resources and actions are available to you that will enable you to progress to your next level.

This sixth driver is about growing your interdependence, which is the sign of a maturing and successful business. I liken the process to the stages of childhood, teenagerhood, and adulthood. Children start out as highly dependent on their parent(s) and family for the necessaries of life; the parent guides them and helps them learn and grow as they navigate their environment. As the child enters the teen years, they rely less on their parents' support and guidance; they experiment with a lot of stuff and are more influenced by peer pressure as they find and test their independence. Eventually, they mature into responsible adults who generally have respectful, amicable relationships with their parent(s)—in essence, a state of interdependence.

So, let's look at this parallel maturity journey that franchisees must travel as they ramp up their business, achieve stability, and eventually reach a point where their business's performance is reflective of their franchisee's hard work and the degree to which they and their franchisor support team have come together.

The Maturity Journey

As you discovered in the previous chapter, every franchisee on the planet will go through a three-phase learning journey through the course of their tenure as a franchisee. There are three phases to the maturation journey as well. While the timing and pace of these journeys are closely parallel, they are two very different processes.

Where the learning journey is focused on acquiring, building and applying knowledge, the maturity journey is about applying awareness, intent and action to how you build, evolve and leverage your relationship with your franchisor.

Progression through the maturity journey does not solely rest with the franchisee, because all parties have to be willing to work at building the relationship—an aspect of which is remaining objective enough to listen and see things from the other's point of view. Communicating at a high and consistent level is not a given, but the TPFs make use of their franchisor's experience and wisdom.

As you digest the insights in this chapter, it's important to understand the "power versus influence" relationship between the franchisor and the franchisee. I chose the word "influence" deliberately. Most franchisors cannot entirely control the franchisee's behavior because the franchisee is an independent business owner. Yes, there is a formal control structure which resides within the franchise agreement and the operations manual, and the franchisee is obligated to follow the rules as defined. Because it's their independent business, though, they can choose not to follow the rules—which may come with great risk, including losing their franchise.

So instead of controlling franchisees' behavior, the franchisor influences it through initial training, early coaching, and ongoing development. The franchisor strives to guide the new franchisee's learning curve in order to build desirable habits that focus on following the system.

This is one of those areas where the strength and weakness of franchising intersects. The franchisor has the proven systems and processes, but the franchisee may choose to ignore elements of them, however unwise. This is why it is important to understand the dynamics of the relationship between franchisee and franchisor, and understand how that relationship matures. And that's not just at the beginning but throughout the entire relationship, for as you'll see, it's in the later stages of relationship maturity when the franchisee has the opportunity to derive the greatest value and benefit of the franchise system—if they choose to leverage it. And part of this maturation journey requires that franchisees must be open to learning and doing things as prescribed by the franchisor, because seldom is a system or process static. Jania Bailey, CEO of FranNet, shares this perspective:

> You've got to constantly be looking for what changes need to be made. You [the franchisee] cannot sit still and expect things to just continue, because the world's changing around us. And if we [franchise owners] become brittle and unwilling to make those adjustments and changes, we'll be left behind. And franchisees who fight that kind of change [will be left behind], because every system evolves. Whether it's their branding, some of their processes, new technology, you have to embrace those things.

The way the franchisee approaches learning the system in the early days sets the foundation for the relationship. Now if you're a more tenured franchisee and happy with your relationship, there are likely still some areas of opportunity to strengthen your relationship with your franchisor that can help take your business to the next level. Or you might be a franchisee who feels like your relationship with your franchisor is less than stellar, but that doesn't mean it always has to be this way. Perhaps you're at a stage of the growth journey where you need to strengthen or maybe even rebuild your relationship with your franchisor. Keep an open mind.

From a franchisor's perspective on learning, Mary Thompson explained to me, "One of our values is looking to the system for correction, proposing all possible solutions, if something is not working. We tell our business coaches, 'As soon as you're a franchise owner saying "This is not working," don't assume that it's not working just because something's broken. Go back and figure out what part of the system they are missing first.' Ninety-five percent of the time, it's something they've forgotten or stopped doing, or didn't think it was a big deal, and it's affecting them further down the line."

Look at this last sentence and ask yourself which of these three (forgotten, stopped doing, not important enough to do) you might be experiencing. Let's get into things to help you identify where you are in your maturity journey.

CHILDHOOD: THE DEPENDENT FRANCHISEE

For much of the first twelve months, new franchisees are highly dependent on their franchisor as they learn the system—how to hire and train their staff; how to find, market to and get customers, etc. They have bought into a franchise and believe that the franchisor is relatively knowledgeable and farsighted when it comes to helping them get their business set up, open, and on the path towards achieving their financial and lifestyle goals. They have committed to listening to and following the franchisor's guidance as they start building their new business. It is in their best interest to communicate with their franchisor often and to be transparent about what they do and don't understand, so that the franchisor can continue to guide them and help them learn the foundation processes and habits we discussed in the last chapter.

As the franchisee progresses into the second year, this next twelve months is akin to the latter stages of childhood. They've made some mistakes, they've enjoyed some successes, and they've learned some components of the system well, but haven't yet gotten to others. They should be past the perception that they'll just open the doors and customers will come; instead, they recognize that the driving of their business is their responsibility, not the franchisor's. They are likely still following much of the franchisor's guidance, but have definitely found the areas where they have some operational latitude.

A small percentage of younger franchisees that resist direction from the franchisor tend to gravitate to those areas of operational latitude, even if operating there doesn't serve them very well. Often it's what Mary Thompson showed us in the last chapter—some franchisees will say "I believe in the system," but don't take any action. And others are taking action, but these actions diverge from the system's procedures. The impact of this latter kind of behavior not only opens the doors to undesirable habits, but, if the behavior isn't brought back to what the system norms require, it also creates roadblocks to future growth and opportunity because the franchisee won't be able to accomplish all the tasks required to sustain that opportunity.

From a relationship-building perspective, any time during the dependent stage that behavior and performance are not what is desired or expected is when courageous conversations need to take place between the franchisor and the franchisee. It's about being willing to be vulnerable, and about communicating with the intent to help each other grow. And it's not always the franchisee who's dropped the ball. Both sides have to be committed first to a) growing together, listening and understanding, and then b) addressing the behaviors and actions/inactions that contributed to the situation. And then both sides need to take the agreed-upon actions and follow up on progress.

I hope you're getting a sense of the trust-building that's an integral component in the dependent stage. The weaker the bond is built, the more likely it is to erode or even disappear in the next maturity phase, independence.

TEENAGERHOOD: THE INDEPENDENT FRANCHISEE

This is where the vast majority of franchisees live, so don't be surprised if you see some of your own patterns here.

As franchisees get past *learning* the system and start *knowing* it, usually around the two-year mark, they shift from being dependent on the franchisor to being an independent franchisee. They have entered the "full stride" phase of their business, where they should be starting to earn moderate to good profitability. This phase can and often does last for many years.

Franchisees in this stage no longer need, or often want, the close attention of their franchisor. They are seeking moderate operational latitude, which involves bringing in their own ideas about how to run the business (better), even if it's off-model. When going off-model, the franchisee's confidence in the business acumen of the franchisor may decline, because they perceive that the franchisor has not been able to deliver on all of the expectations the franchisee initially had, even if some of them were unrealistic.

At some point in this independence phase, it's natural for franchisees to start questioning the value they're getting from the royalties they're paying to their franchisor, and many do. It's also common for franchisees at this stage to forget "who took them to the dance." They see their success as their own making, and attribute less of it to the franchisor's business model and the coaching, training and support that they received during their ramp-up stage.

Like the maturing teenager, in the middle to late stage of the independence phase the maturing franchisees soften some of their negative perceptions of, and resistance toward, their franchisor. They've made enough mistakes by going off-process or by missing opportunities because they didn't pay attention to the coaching and advice. They look in the mirror and understand that, "Yeah, I'm at my current level because of the decisions I made and because of the actions I took/didn't take, and *not* because of what the franchisor did/didn't do." They begin to see greater value in the systems, support, and the royalty dollars they pay. And they start drawing on additional resources their franchisor and the system have to offer.

From a relationship management perspective, entering this phase is a critical time for the franchisee. The dependence on the franchisor has waned, but the franchisee is still developing and most will want to be part of a group that will align with their point of view, so they are also building their relationships with peer franchisees. Like a teenager and the peer groups they join, the choices the franchisee makes about which peer franchisees they build relationships with often has direct impact on their growth and success levels.

Here's a bit more of Jania Bailey's perspective:

Franchisees also have to be self-reliant and self-motivated. They need to be able to get up and get going without somebody telling them to do that. Franchisees set their own goals, and define how their day, week, and month is going to be. Being self-reliant means, "I can do this on my own, I've got the structure and the process provided by the franchisor, the support there, but I don't need them to come in here and run my business for me."

It's [building] that interdependence we talk about so much in franchising. And realizing that, but also realizing, what's my part that I have to do that nobody can fix for me, that self-motivation. I find people who have a positive attitude also motivate themselves.

....

Franchisors are focused on continually building and optimizing the systems and processes, and often play more of a sounding board or coach role during this phase, where they help the franchisee to become aware of the various tools and resources available to them as they achieve progressive growth milestones— to the degree that the franchisee wants that level of support.

....

ADULTHOOD: THE INTERDEPENDENT FRANCHISEE

Franchisees that transition into this interdependence stage are often in influencer or even mentor roles with newer franchisees because they understand the strength of the systems and want to see more of their peers improve. They have mastered many elements of the franchisor's business systems because they have learned through much trial and error that going too far off-system doesn't work. Yes, they innovate, but do so with the franchisor's input and support. They regularly share best practices with peer franchisees, and often work closely with their franchisor on special projects or pilot initiatives (e.g., menu or process innovations and new marketing methods) for the betterment of the operational systems and the brand.

Franchisees at this stage enjoy rich relationships with their franchisor because they and their franchisor respect and understand each other's perspectives and goals; they communicate openly about opportunities and challenges alike. They often have a seat at the franchisor's strategy discussion table or serve on the franchisee advisory council. Sarosh Nayar, a franchisee with FASTSIGNS, describes what it is like to be working collaboratively with other TPFs and the franchisor:

> We have board groups that we're a part of. A lot of the top-performing franchisees want to be part of the board group where we get together with other like-minded franchisees and we dissect our business plans and challenge each other and challenge assumptions. We try to motivate each other to grow and to be better... The plan is something that we present, not only to the board group, but to our employees so we can illustrate to them where we want to be and what we want to do. We go through it quarterly and we update where we are versus our plan. In a lot of ways, it's not different from what a large corporation does... So, it is bringing that culture of a larger company and the bigger mindset to a small business.

It might sound like these franchisees are the easiest relationships for the franchisor to manage, but they are not. These franchisees have the highest expectations of their franchisor, right-fully placed, and hold the franchisor accountable to work together to resolve system challenges and anticipate future opportunities or threats, then prepare for those. These franchisees are great con-nectors within the brand and big advocates of participating in the franchisor's conferences.

As a result, interdependent franchisees are often in the top 25 percent of performers in any franchise brand, as they derive max-imum value from the brand, from the systems, and from the fran-chisor's knowledge and resources. Interdependent franchisees seek out and actively engage with other top franchisees, and challenge each other to excel even further, as evidenced by Sarosh. Because of that, the average royalty revenue and knowledge contribution gen-erated for the franchisor are disproportionately tilted in favor of the top 25 percent of franchisees—those who have discovered how to strike the interdependence relationship. No wonder it is in every-one's best interest to work toward interdependence.

With all that being said, it might come as a shock that relatively few franchisees transition fully into the interdependent stage. Part of this is because the independent stage of franchise ownership provides enough financial and lifestyle comfort that many franchi-sees don't think to put more effort into progressing further. They are good franchisees, with good businesses that drive results that keep them happy enough.

But let me bring in some sage advice from Charles Bonfiglio in case anyone is leaning towards complacency: "Quite frankly, if you're not growing, you're shrinking. You're either going up the ladder or you're going down. The idea is you have to work on your business every day. Things change. Employees evolve. You have to pay attention to what's in the business, around the business, and its growth. Don't ever think it's like, 'When I get to this level, I'm good with that one store.'"

Let me reiterate what I opened this chapter with: the significance of transitioning from the independent stage to interdependent was one of the most important things that I did not see coming when I set out on my research journey for this book. Without exception, every single top-performing franchisee I interviewed demonstrated the mindset and all the qualities of having an interdependent relationship with their franchisor. I did not encounter a single top performer who demonstrated only an independent-stage mindset.

GROWTH PLAN EXERCISE 7-1
Where are you and where are you headed?

Take a few minutes to reflect on where you currently are on your maturity journey, and where you are headed.

PART A: Growth Trajectory Analysis
- Is your trajectory flat, indicating some level of being stuck?
- Is your trajectory gently increasing or might it be aggressively increasing?
- Or is it declining?
- What's happening in your business that's impacting your trajectory?

PART B: Forces Analysis
From the assessment zone exercises in chapter 3:
- What internal forces are at play?
- What external forces are at play?
- How might you and your team be able to respond to these forces?

PART C: Analysis of Your Activities
- What might have you accepted (erroneously?) about your franchisor's desire and willingness to support your progress?
- How much have you resisted following the system as it is intended to be followed, or even rebelled against the direction your franchisor has previously attempted to provide? Which parts of the system do you resist the most?
- How much are your current results being influenced by your actions and leadership, or lack thereof?
- What skills do you need to work on to advance to your next level?
- What skills do you need to get your team members to work on to advance to their next level?

Self-Limiting Beliefs and Becoming Unstuck

What did you find when you completed the last exercise? Is your performance on a pace and trajectory you're comfortable with? Is your franchisee maturity level where you thought it was? Do you understand where you want to go and how you will get there?

My guess is that some of you are already well on your way to interdependence, and others, well, you might be stuck. Before you can become unstuck, it's important to recognize and acknowledge what is keeping you stuck in the first place. Is this one of those moments in your life when you realize that the only way to improve your circumstances, to get past where you are, is solely up to you? Cynthia Keenan says underperforming franchisees "tell themselves the reasons why it can't be as opposed to focusing on what *can* be."

We're all guilty from time to time of telling ourselves why something can't be. Top performers aren't immune to this either. However, what I've come to understand is that TPFs don't wallow in that quagmire of what can't be; they look for answers regarding what *is* possible, and then work to understand how they might be able to achieve it. When talking about why some franchisees may be stuck, David Druker offers this perspective:

> For one reason or another, [some franchisees] lose their relationship to the operational standards or imperatives of the business that attracted them to it in the first place. The same things that made it interesting for them when they got into the franchise and stroked the check, [such as] "I want to be part of this brand family because they do it really well. And [others have] learned from experience. I love the fact that this is a twenty-five-year-old brand, a ten-year-old brand. I love the fact that someone else has been on the bleeding edge before me and I don't have to take those cuts myself."
>
> And then something seems to click somewhere when they get to this middle area where they think: "I'm no longer at the bottom of the list. So I'm doing really good. And [getting into the top group] just seems so far away that I'm not really sure how to get there. And I'm kind of embarrassed to ask the questions."

What operational imperatives—the franchisor's systems and processes—might you have lost your relationship with? Which ones might you never have started a relationship with?

What questions might you be afraid of asking? What resources are available to help you and your team get precise, relevant answers that can help your business advance, immediately? Look at what Doug Brauer has to say about leveraging the collective brain trust:

> I think everybody should participate. You can learn a lot. You can talk to other franchisees, listen to what they're going through. Listen to the top ones. It's always nice to pick out some of the up-and-coming guys that are really aggressive and listen to what they're going through or where they're having successes. I also believe it's very important that your employees, your top employees—that could be like a production manager, sales manager, sales staff—need to participate in this stuff too.

ACCESS THE COLLECTIVE BRAIN TRUST

Vanessa Yakobson offers her perspective on her own franchisees and the resources available to them:

> You can't have a defeatist attitude as an entrepreneur. You have to believe in your ability to overcome and your ability to identify where the resources and tools are. It's not only about looking to yourself for the answers. So, often I'll say to a franchise partner, "Well, have you reached out to other franchise partners to see what's worked for them or how they overcame that challenge?" And I'm always surprised when they haven't. As a franchisee, you've got this amazing resource—a built-in peer group for mentorship and collaboration. It's actually surprising to me when people aren't really taking advantage of that. So that resourcefulness is part of that can-do attitude—"I'm going to find out more. I know there are resources out there and I'm going to look for them."

Let's look at some of the collective brain trust resources within your system that TPFs often leverage. As you read through these, start identifying which are available to you and consider what your next steps might be on your path to next-level growth. How might those steps fit into your personal and business growth plan?

While every franchise system is different, and while each franchisor has their own culture for acquiring, refining, and sharing accumulated knowledge and experiences of their franchisees, there are many ways a franchisee can access this information, whether it's already part of a formal sharing structure or not. Franchisees that are focused on figuring out how to get to the next level are willing to ask for guidance or help. To quote Greg Nathan of the Franchise Relationships Institute, "You can't get to the top if you don't have good mentors and good support." However, he continues with a good warning, "You can have the best advisers and stuff and still [an] ego can get in the way [by saying], 'Well, I know better.'"

While the focus here is on gaining knowledge and specific ideas from several identified sources, here are a handful of examples available to you:

- annual conferences and regional meetings
- franchisee to franchisee accountability calls (monthly challenge team call)
- call a friend (franchisee to franchisee mentoring and visiting other franchisees)
- franchisee mastermind groups
- monthly content calls, intranet, video library, Facebook groups
- working with your field business coach

ANNUAL CONFERENCES

Annual meetings are among the most critical events that a franchisee can attend in the calendar year. This is where franchisors and franchisees come together to cover relevant topics like emerging trends and technology advances, and changes in their customers' behavior.

Cynthia Keenan places a lot of value on personal connection. She told me: "The annual meetings [provide] the opportunity to connect with other people in the same business facing the same challenges; you always gain something from it. And even when you have a group of peers who are equally successful, it's the opportunity to sit down and say, 'Oh, we did this, have you ever tried that?' It fuels your creativity in your own business. I think that's invaluable."

I'm always disheartened when I hear of franchisor conferences where only 65 to 75 percent of the franchisee base attends. My belief is that when franchisees choose not to attend, it's because they look at the agenda and the planned meeting content, and they base their decision not to attend on that agenda. This is unfortunate, because they're missing the biggest reason for attending, which is getting onto the biggest access ramp to the collective brain trust. Conferences and meetings are more about building stronger relationships with peers, suppliers, and the franchisor's leadership team than they are about seeing content presentations.

Don Elliott offers this perspective: "I think the best part about the franchising piece and Great Clips, of course, is networking with all the other franchisees... We learn a lot more from those folks than what maybe even Great Clips can teach us. That ability to get to those conventions, and zone meetings, and all the different things, that networking is huge."

Brad Rush is bullish on connecting with peers at conferences: "Conferences are good, but the substance from the conference coming from corporate is not a game changer. They're updates on growth and things along those lines, but all the value from the conference comes from those one-off interactions or those group interactions with other owners. It's having those private dinners and talking about challenges you're going through in your market. And then having someone else who has gone through those exact same challenges tell you how they got through them, how they overcome them, how they're better because of what they did."

What Brad is talking about here is exactly the point I'm striving to drive home for you in this chapter: the incredible value in sitting down with other people who are running the same business as you and being fearless enough to *ask questions* to get other people's perspectives on how to overcome some of the challenges you're facing, and on how to capitalize on some of the opportunities in front of you.

While it's great to get ideas from the conferences and other franchisees, if when you get back to your business you try to implement too many things, or worse, you don't implement anything, well, that's a big squandering of knowledge, time and money. Yes, a core objective for attending these meetings is to get ideas, so how can you get the most out of attending? Here's a bit of further insight from Don Elliott:

> We go to a Great Clips function and we're sitting through some of their presentations, writing down all these notes, and the guy that isn't organized or doesn't know what he's doing, he's going to go back [to his business] and he's going to spill all this stuff on the table, and he's going to try to do a hundred different things, and he's not going to be successful with any of them.
>
> Narrow it down. Focus to find one or two nuggets, and then just lock in on that thing, and get that implemented in your business, and get it to be kind of a standard part of your business—part of your operations—and then grab the next one, and just keep adding and building your business from there.

In this one key observation Don captured the essence of the Growth Helix—master the knowledge at the core and grow through experimenting around the edges. The experimenting is to find those nuggets and get them implemented in your business. When those nuggets become a standard part of your operations, you create momentum and are ready to power up to the next level, embrace the next learning opportunity, and keep climbing.

FRANCHISEE TO FRANCHISEE ACCOUNTABILITY CALLS

Mutual accountability calls are one of the best ways for franchises to stay focused on their growth goals. These are usually thirty- to sixty-minute calls that are held at regular intervals (e.g., bi-weekly or monthly), where goals, ideas to achieve those goals, and progress made toward completing them are discussed. Often, friendly competition becomes a bit of a catalyst to help keep the focus in between calls. Having too many people on these calls actually works against the intended outcome, so I recommend groups of two or three people so that each person has enough of an opportunity to contribute.

CALLS AND VISITS

Picking up the phone or getting on a video call with an experienced franchisee is a great way to get insights on how to approach an opportunity or challenge. Think of the benefit of learning from someone who has been around the block a few times and can really compress your learning curve. Experienced franchisees welcome the opportunity to help their peer franchisees out because they recognize that helping others to make improvements is also of benefit to the franchise system. Sometimes this includes visiting another franchisee's location to see how they do things differently. Jared Rothberger shares this:

> Most of my success I credit to things that I've taken from other markets. I made it a point to visit other Jan-Pro markets early on, so that I could see what they're doing, what they're doing well, and what they're struggling with, and kind of better understand what I can bring back to Detroit.
>
> As I walk through my office, I'm sure I could point out ten different things that are taken from other markets. And we've contributed some of those that have been taken from Detroit and spread around the country. I'm proud of those as well. But I credit most of the success [to learning] things from other people. I mean, they freely give [the input].

Jared alludes to another important factor, which is that some more experienced franchisees even offer to become mentors to newer franchisees; all you have to do is ask for their help and be willing to do some of what they suggest. I credit much of my early success in my FranNet business with asking five of the top franchisees at the time to mentor me, each on a different area of my business. That mentoring enabled me to have the third-fastest start in FranNet's then seventeen-year history. This is another reason why attending conferences is so important, because it's one of the best opportunities to build relationships with more experienced franchisees.

FRANCHISEE MASTERMIND GROUPS

Mastermind groups take accountability calls to the next level. These groups are one of the most powerful resources available to drive operational excellence, but members have to be willing to be transparent enough to share vital information. Franchisees in these groups usually get together quarterly or semi-annually for several hours to do a deeper dive into what's going on in their business. A typical format is that each member of these groups starts by reporting on progress with commitments they made on specific challenges or opportunities at the previous meeting, and then shares what they're facing for the coming quarter and gets the group's input on what additional actions they might be able to take. Each franchisee then commits to specific new actions that they'll report on at the next meeting. Some groups (especially top-performer mastermind groups) get really deep and get into sharing of KPIs and profitability information.

MONTHLY CONTENT CALLS, INTRANET, VIDEO LIBRARY

Franchisors offer a plethora of resources that have been built over the years, and yes, some franchisors are far better at curating these resources than others. Many of these resources can be found on the franchisor's intranet. Video training resources are especially helpful for newer franchisees; these can include things like dedicated content calls, which are held periodically and recorded for ongoing reference and focus on topics like best practice presentations, marketing or operations. Even weekly updates are a great resource for staying up to date and grabbing ideas that franchisees are using to drive new business, improve profitability, etc. As Dan Monaghan said, it's important that franchisees pay attention to how and what their franchisor communicates, and they have to remain in sync with the franchisor to be aware of changes to the business.

WORKING WITH YOUR FIELD BUSINESS COACH

The franchisor's field business coach (FBC) is the individual responsible for supporting and coaching the franchisees; they play an integral role in the franchisees' success. With more mature franchise systems, there will likely be a team of FBCs dedicated to only this role, whereas with younger systems, the individuals in the FBC role will likely have split duties; they could even be the franchise system's founder(s) or senior executives.

The primary advantage of the FBC is that they bring the broad-range perspective and experience of working with multiple franchisees in multiple markets, enabling them to see what's working and not working across a spectrum of environments. This enables them to see current/approaching problems and opportunities that franchisees might not see, or as is more often the case, might not want to look at or acknowledge.

These FBCs are often thought of by franchisees as either coaches or cops. The cop part of the role is to ensure compliance with operational standards and to issue warnings and report defaults when necessary. As coaches and advisers to the franchisees, FBCs can be one of the most instrumental and impactful resources available to newcomers, and to seasoned franchisees who are striving to overcome challenges or achieve some next-level growth target. Great FBCs are skilled observers and communicators. They strive to understand the franchisee's financial and lifestyle goals, and what the contributing factors to their current circumstances are, then they draw upon their wider perspective to provide guidance that helps the franchisee make the desired real-time progress, both in terms of operational improvement and personal skills development. Franchisees must be willing to communicate openly enough with the FBC about their challenges or unrealized opportunities for the relationship to be beneficial. Building mutual trust over time is an important component of the FBC-franchisee relationship.

As an aside, by completing the surveys and exercises in this book, what you discover might serve as a great reconnecting point with your FBC.

Contributing to the Collective Brain Trust

The franchise business model would not exist as it does today if franchisors and franchisees did not constantly contribute ideas, time, and even money to the betterment of the systems and processes. As I shared earlier in this chapter, interdependence is the highest state of maturity that franchisees achieve, and a big part of that maturity is the willingness to be transparent and share knowledge and experience with their franchisor and with other franchisees in their system.

Ultimately, success in franchise ownership is not just about drawing from the system—it's also about contributing back, and doing so on an ongoing basis, because it's this sharing that helps everyone continue on their journey towards achieving operational excellence. Here's what Dan Monaghan offers:

> In franchising, we have this network effect, where a franchise system with fifty or one hundred franchisees learns so much faster. Our only competitive advantage in today's world is the speed at which we learn. And if the franchisor is wired correctly, it becomes a learning organization. Which means that they're constantly on the lookout for the innovations that are happening in the system.
>
> And in this world, the power comes from everyone sharing. Because that gives us competitive advantage if we're moving faster than our competitors and if we're learning faster than our competitors. And so, a new idea could emerge anywhere within the system. What that means is you're going to constantly be getting new ideas and the system's going to constantly be evolving. But you also have to be a contributor to that. And everyone has different strengths and weaknesses, and things they bring to the table. But that is an important success trait—the willingness to share.
>
> And understanding that we're not competing against our other franchisees—we're a team. Every success in that system increases the value of the brand. So I think collaboration is a key characteristic. Curiosity is really important, because you're going to constantly be learning from the customer. You're going to be learning from the competition. You're going to be learning from your peers.

And some of those things are going to be things you adopt into your business. Some of them are going to be things that you bring to the network. But, we find that some of the highest performers are people that are bringing new ideas to the table.

Doug Phillip, president of Budget Blinds, believes in building a strong culture by prioritizing learning: "Whether or not you're in a franchise organization, or just run a small business, there are many opportunities to engage with others about what they're doing and how they're doing it. These are opportunities for people to learn and think differently about their day-to-day business and how to get better. I think that is incredibly important for people to understand in what they're doing."

A FINAL THOUGHT on achieving the interdependence phase of maturity is that franchisees who have achieved this level typically have businesses that are very saleable and so will earn the highest price at time of sale, because a) these owners are focused on operational excellence *and* growth (two important determinants in business valuation), and b) these businesses do not rely solely on the owner to run the day-to-day interactions with the customers. Think of it this way: the less the owner is the visible face of the business, the easier it is to find a buyer, and the easier it is for the new owner to take the reins of the new business.

How does a franchisee know when they've "arrived," or when their business is meeting and exceeding all of their goals, or when it is marketable enough for resale that buyers will line up for the opportunity? Uniformly across the interviews, the mantra for understanding the health of the business was "know your numbers." What do top performers do? Doug Phillip says, "You get to that top group, they measure everything throughout their organization and clearly understand what the drivers and the motivators are for their team to make a difference and get to that next level. And I think that's incredibly important." In the next chapter, we look at the ways top performers measure and track success, and what steps they take when the numbers aren't pretty.

Before you move on to chapter 8, be sure to complete the survey.

SURVEY 7-1:
How Would I Assess Progress along My Maturity Journey?

Respond to the statements below on a scale of 1 (rarely) to 5 (always).	1	2	3	4	5
I take the time to assess the quality of interactions with my franchisor on a regular basis.					
I am 100% committed to a productive relationship with my franchisor.					
I implement the coaching and training I receive from my franchisor.					
There are times when I think my franchisor is less committed to my success than I am, and that is frustrating.					
There are times when my franchisor has suggested I need to step up my game and make better use of resources I have at my disposal.					
I understand how business works and I am open to innovating my business from time to time.					
I would describe the relationship with my franchisor as one of mutual accountability.					
I believe I derive maximum benefit from my franchisor's brand and systems.					
I am open to working with fellow franchisees to compare notes and take and offer constructive input instead of destructive criticism.					
I constantly set next-level growth targets.					
I am never complacent about my business.					
When my business increases or decreases, I investigate the factors that are influencing the trajectory.					

Respond to the statements below on a scale of 1 (rarely) to 5 (always).	1	2	3	4	5
I take full accountability for downturns in my business. There is no one to "blame."					
I constantly coach my team to scale up the business.					
I attend conferences, either in person or online.					
I attend peer group sessions.					
I believe that franchisees have a collective knowledge that surpasses the franchisor's coaching and training.					
I assess ideas and information, and prioritize any items that can have a benefit for the business.					
I participate in accountability groups.					
I understand the value of experience and what I stand to gain from learning from other franchisees, and also sharing what I know.					

YOUR SCORE: What do your ratings tell you about where you are on your maturity journey? Can you identify areas that would lead you to progress faster along that journey?

Driver No. 6 Takeaways

List your top three takeaways from this chapter:

1. _____

2. _____

3. _____

CHAPTER 8

DRIVER NO. 7
Cultivate the Neural
Network of Your Business

ONE THING THAT'S EMPHASIZED in every good business book is the importance of tracking and measuring progress and results. While the authors might vary slightly in how they define what gets measured and how to measure it, the broadly accepted terminology about what to measure is Key Performance Indicators, or KPIs. Another frequently used term is "knowing your numbers." Joel Winters gave me his insights into awareness around numbers:

> Not knowing your numbers [means] thinking you're in a different place than you are. Something as simple as job costing or understanding your true cost of goods and your gross profit, let alone net profit, but just even the ability to understand your gross profit. I think sometimes what can happen is the money can start flowing in because you did the marketing piece right and you're acquiring customers, but if you don't really understand those numbers, then you're going to have a false sense of security potentially, and then

you're going to make bad decisions. It's all very interrelated, but I do think people that aren't at the top may have a false sense of security around their numbers by not knowing them.

Stuart Burns, the president of SpeedPro Graphics, links numbers to performance: "Top performers are very aware of their numbers. They are competitive and goal focused. Top performers pay attention. Middle performers get things half done."

On a scale of 1 to 10, how closely do Joel's and Stuart's comments describe you? Are you more of a top performer or a middle performer?

What first comes to mind for most business owners when they hear "know the numbers" is profitability, bank balance, and cash flow. Many are intimidated by their lack of financial savvy and rely on their bookkeeper to input the weekly or monthly financial data and engage professional accountants to prepare their financial statements at the end of the year. They believe that this activity amounts to understanding the health of their business. They can't be more wrong.

As I outlined in chapter 4, financial information is only one component of the information that every business owner needs to monitor to be able to assess their business's performance. And yes, it is a very important component, but financial information is simply a look back at what has already happened. It's a look in the rear-view mirror. Such information cannot be a reliable predictor of how well your business will do going forward. And looking forward is necessary for sustaining growth and success. I can tell you from experience that far too many entrepreneurs and franchisees fail to understand this critical factor.

Key Performance Indicators:
The Neural Network of Your Business

To be able to effectively assess future performance, you will need and want to manage your current activities with a broader set of operational data points or values. These will form the basis of your KPIs, and will vary depending on the nature of your franchise. Understanding which KPIs are important and relevant will enable you to acquire and assess vital information about the current state of your operation. The higher the quality and relevance of the information, the better your decisions will be.

KPI.org defines KPIs as "critical (key) indicators of progress toward an intended result. KPIs provide a focus for strategic and operational improvement, create an analytical basis for decision-making and help focus attention on what matters most." As author Peter Drucker famously said, "What gets measured gets done."

KPI.org states the following about KPIs:

> The relative business intelligence value of a set of measurements is greatly improved when the organization [e.g., the franchisee's business] understands how various metrics are used and how different types of measures contribute to the picture of how the organization is doing. KPIs can be categorized into several different types. Here are some of the main ones:
> - Inputs measure attributes (amount, type, quality) of resources consumed in processes that produce outputs
> - Process or activity measures focus on how the efficiency, quality, or consistency of specific processes [are] used to produce a specific output; they can also measure controls on that process, such as the tools/equipment used or process training
> - Outputs are result measures that indicate how much work is done and define what is produced
> - Outcomes focus on accomplishments or impacts, and are classified as Intermediate Outcomes, such as customer brand awareness (a direct result of, say, marketing or communications outputs), or End Outcomes, such as customer retention or sales (that are driven by the increased brand awareness)
> - Project measures answer questions about the status of deliverables and milestone progress related to important projects or initiatives[20]

It is a lot to think about, and for many it can feel incredibly over-whelming. But it reiterates the need to make the effort to work *on* your business, not *in* your business. For the franchisees that fail to recognize this and do not use KPI data to make decisions, it is likely this very reason they remain stuck at their current level of performance—which is almost always far less than they are capa-ble of accomplishing. Leveraging KPI data doesn't need to be over-whelming and complicated. Let's make understanding and using KPI tracking less daunting. Most KPIs fall into one of two camps—Lag Indicators and Lead Indicators.

- Lag Indicators are results of what has already happened in your business. Once recorded, they cannot be changed or influenced; they are simply a point in the history of your business (e.g., monthly sales totals or average transaction value per customer). Annual financial statements are also lag indicators.

- Lead Indicators are your input elements and activities that define what actions are necessary to achieve your goals, so that you can influence and even forecast future outcomes. For exam-ple, the activities it takes to drive an increase in your level of cus-tomer inflow on a certain day is a lead indicator. In this example, if you can increase the number of customers on any given day, then you should reasonably expect that you will enjoy a higher sales volume. When you take lead indicators and apply them to the inputs from your franchisor's baseline KPI data, that's when they become predictive.

Here's an example of the application of data for a business-to-business service franchise:

Baseline Data Inputs	
Average number of appointments per month for a second-year franchise	24 (6 per week)
Win ratio of franchise	25% of all first appointments (6 wins per month)
Revenue of first sale transaction (an average)	$6,000
Revenue projection per month from 24 client appointments per month	$36,000 ($6,000 x 6 wins)
Revenue projection for 12 months from 24 client appointments per month	$432,000 ($36,000 x 12 months)

Lead indicator activity:

Predictor	
If number of appointments per month is increased from 24 to 40	40 (10 per week)
Win ratio of franchise	25% of all first appointments (10 wins per month)
Revenue of first sale transaction (an average)	$6,000
Revenue projection per month from 40 client appointments per month	$60,000 ($6,000 x 10 wins)
Revenue projection for 12 months from 40 client appointments per month	$720,000 ($60,000 × 12 months)

PREDICTOR: If Jane Franchisee increases her number of appointments from six to ten per week, then provided she's following the franchisor's sales process, she can reasonably predict that her revenue will increase from $432,000 to $720,000.

Sounds easy, right? Well, two additional indicators need to be factored in before the average number of appointments: 1) How many raw leads does it take to have one fully qualified lead? and 2) How many qualified leads does it take to get a client appointment?

Number of raw leads to get 1 client appointment: 5
Number of referred leads to get 1 client appointment: 3
Total: 8 leads produce 2 client appointments
Goal: 40 appointments per month
Number of raw leads required for 20 appointments: 100
Number of referred leads for 20 appointments: 60

In order for Jane Franchisee to get to 40 appointments, she has to get 60 referrals and 100 raw leads, or an equivalent thereof. What is the extra work she has to do? What are the additional lead sources she has to create and nurture to achieve her loftier goal?

You see, it's one thing to do the paper math exercise; it's entirely another to work it backwards and break it down into the originating activity that's required to accomplish the objective. That's what I mean by "predictive." Only once breaking it down to the originating activity is done are you able to identify the time, money, and people resources needed to achieve the goal.

One disadvantage of only relying upon lag indicators is that by the time you get the data, you are only looking at a historical record, and the opportunity to impact the outcome is long past. The primary reason you want to utilize KPIs is so that you can identify where opportunities or challenges exist *now* so that you can take prompt and meaningful action to improve your current and future results. For this reason, it's important to use lead and lag indicators in tandem.

What makes using KPIs intimidating for some is that there are potentially many KPIs that apply to a business, so how do you know which ones to track and measure? If you choose the wrong ones, you will not be tracking the optimal data, and you are burning resources in the meantime.

What's encouraging if you've never used KPIs before is that you don't have to learn how to measure a ton of them. You'll just want to measure the handful that are most relevant to improving whichever parts of your business will have the biggest impact on helping you get from where you are now to where you want to get to next. In other words, *what matters most?* The KPIs you track and measure should be directly relevant to your most immediate growth and business improvement goals.

Vanessa Yakobson links numbers to performance and strategy:

> The ability to go from visioning and ambition—your forward-looking [efforts]—to action involves being able to be strategic. So, what are the skills that you need? You need to know your numbers. What's amazing to me is how many people are so intimidated by their numbers. You so often talk to a franchisee, and they say, "Well, I don't know—I have to check with my bookkeeper, or I have to check with my partner. They're the ones who do the numbers." These aren't complicated businesses. The P&Ls are pretty simple. So, know your numbers and know your benchmarks, so that you can really focus in on what levers you can pull and what areas you should be focusing on. Zero in on those, where you can really move the needle for yourself.
>
> And once you know what those are, manage to those benchmarks. In other words, know where you're at today and what the benchmark is that you want to achieve. Set interim goals along the way if you need to, so that you're not putting pressure on yourself to execute on a giant leap that's not realistic based on where you're at today. And then develop the action plan, and really focus in on what the very specific actionable items and the steps are that you need to take to get from where you are today to that benchmark or goal. Use those numbers to make strategic decisions that help you focus on the big opportunities that are really going to move the needle and then translate that into an action plan.

As the neural network of your business, KPIs are the neurotransmitters of pain and pleasure signals of your business's central nervous system. The more developed you can make your KPI nervous system, the greater the *aware-sense* you'll have of what's going on. You'll be able to more effectively identify the signals, positive or negative, which will then allow you to assess and respond to them.

Like your body, your business's nervous system presents you with signals all the time. Some are painful and others pleasurable. With pain synapses, the more intense the pain, the faster you want to respond, and the more important it is to have really thorough diagnostic capability so that you can take the most appropriate corrective path; you want to reduce its immediate effect. The more intense it is, the more likely you'll learn to avoid the cause of the pain in the future.

With pleasure synapses, the more intense the pleasure, the longer you want it to last, and the more you'll want it again in future. When things go right, like making a big sale or delivering an order that wows your customer, you want to repeat the cause of the pleasure, right? When you figure out what caused the pleasure, you'll likely make a few operational adjustments and build a mini-system that allows you to increase the cause and frequency of that pleasure in the future.

Your lead and lag KPIs are simply the current truth signals from the pain and pleasure sensors of your business. When lead indicator activities are showing that your business is on track with its goals, or may even exceed them, pleasure signals are felt by the team members and transmitted to the franchise owner or the leader/ manager.

Without an effective neural network, when good or bad things happen, you might not even be aware of them happening because there's little transparency as to their causes. They often get masked as something entirely different, and the result is that the franchisee often ends up chasing ghost pains or ghost opportunities, and burning through precious resources in the process. Some franchisees also tend to be scattered and chase the hottest new opportunities (squirrel syndrome) instead of staying focused on the opportunities that the very franchise model they bought is designed to maximize.

On a scale of 1 to 10, how much does this insufficient transparency describe the way you're currently operating your business?

Take a moment to revisit Growth Plan Exercise 3-2: Performance Journey Locator and review your highest-priority growth/challenge areas. How much are each of these caused by gaps in information about why they are happening? Which shadow pains and pleasures might you be chasing?

The KPI data is like an ongoing MRI scan that is readily and constantly available. Once you've learned how to understand the information, you and your team can access it at any time to make faster, better diagnoses, and then make more informed decisions.

Colin Bates offers this method for keeping everything and everyone connected to the KPI data:

> You have to have KPIs. We just did our month-end. Each of my offices has their own scorecard, all the same metrics that we're tracking, different objectives, based on where they are in life cycle and where they are inside the territory. Each of my regional directors will go through their results, speak to those results. We even color code. Green is good. Red is not so good. They'll speak to those results, [and] if they didn't meet objectives, they'll need to identify what to do differently this coming month to better those results.
>
> Again, we know what the levers are for growth in the business. That's our prime objective—growth. You've got to have retention. You've got to have sales. You have to have those two working in unison. It's not enough that you can sell remarkable amounts with it all going out the back door [by not managing profitability]. You have to have both pieces working. Then you have to be able to collect on the bills as well. You got to do that in a timely fashion.
>
> Then, at the end of the year, we look at what the trends and patterns of our business were.

GROWTH PLAN EXERCISE 8-1
What KPIs are you using? Are they the right ones?

Recall KPI.org's point that KPIs "help focus attention on what matters most." For this exercise, I ask you to identify which business activities and functions matter most to you, your team, and your business. There's a survey coming up that is a complement to this exercise, so please complete this first.

- What KPIs are you currently using in your business?
- How certain are you that they are the right KPIs?
- How frequently are you looking at your KPIs?
- How does the information you get from your KPIs shape your decisions?

If you're already tracking and measuring KPIs in your business, congratulations. This is a good time to ask yourself if you're getting enough critical data to make optimal decisions. Is it time to expand your KPI scorecard?

If you conclude that you and your team need to assess how to bring more robust KPI tracking and measuring into your decision-making, then you have taken a major step forward in that you have recognized the need to improve the quality of your data. Now is the time to figure out your next steps, which will improve the quality of your decisions. As Vanessa Yakobson points out, forward-looking action is strategic.

What's exciting is that one of the great benefits of being part of a franchise system is this: most franchisors know the core KPIs that drive their business model, and they strive to communicate to their franchisees about the importance of the data that the KPI measures provide. Your franchisor might even have dedicated franchisee support staff to help accelerate this learning and adopt it as a core habit going forward. Catherine Monson coaches her franchisees this way:

Focus on Key Performance Indicators. That's going to include some financial statement KPIs and non-financial KPIs such as Net Promoter Score, the number of re-dos, or the closing rate on quotes. What is the actual quote-to-order rate? If it's at a hundred percent, your prices are probably too low. If it's 5 percent, something's wrong. So what do we need to do? Those kinds of KPIs are very important, just as are the key financial KPIs. We judge franchisee performance by how they continually grow sales and profits. That's how we use the criteria. We think that's the most objective criteria for any business owner—sales and profits.

If you're never reviewing your financial statements, you don't know how you're doing until you run out of money, or you file your tax returns. We recommend our franchisees review their financial statements every month and keep their financial statements using the accrual method.

Ask your franchisor or top franchisees in your system to help you get a better handle on which KPIs are the most critical, and for some direction on how to access and understand this information. As you get more adept with leveraging KPI data, you can take things to the next level by having more robust discussions with the TPFs in your system about which KPIs they pay close attention to, and more importantly, how they use this information to guide their decisions.

The nature of their business dictated the degree of complexity of the available data involved in "knowing their numbers," but every one of the TPFs had clarity on the critical numbers that mattered in their business; more importantly, every one of them looked at and leveraged that data at least weekly, and in some cases, daily.

Linking Goals and KPIs

Another critical component of the neural network of your business is having clearly defined goals and objectives, because without clear targets, KPI data becomes far less useful. Greg Nathan made this comment on goals and top performers: "A really, really successful franchisee, if you have a conversation with them about what they are working on [and] what their goals are, they're very clear. They'll say, 'I'm looking to expand my sales by 17 percent over the next six months.' Or, 'I'm going to put in another customer service area.' Or, 'I'm going to restructure my team.' So it's that clarity around goals at a very practical level."

Cynthia Keenan says that even though she believes success isn't solely based on numbers, she believes in the synergy between KPIs and goal setting:

> I always tell people, "A goal not set is a goal not met." And a goal is really just an analysis tool. I find people are afraid to set goals because they're afraid they're not going to reach them. What if they're not good enough? I feel they might surprise themselves that not only are they good enough, but they're better than a lot of other people when they start really tracking things. And when they set goals and they don't meet them, or they're not where they want to be, that's really the marker to look at and really get in-depth about: "Why isn't it working? And should I try a different tactic?" You know, [having KPIs that inform your goals creates] a place where a problem can be solved. And if you don't have that number to look at, you don't even know the problem really exists.

When norm-based KPI data are available (e.g., system-average performance ratios like sales conversion ratios, production time, or food costs), the importance of having some goals focused on achieving or beating those ratios helps the business to progress to higher levels of operational excellence. As Peter Drucker famously said, "A strategy without metrics is just a wish. And metrics that are not aligned with strategic objectives are a waste of time."

Greg Nathan adds this: "I call [goal setting] vision because it's being able to visualize what you want... and then you take the action. But, just doing action without being clear on what you're trying to do is a bit of a bull in the china shop, isn't it?

"So, it comes down to good judgment. What we're talking about is the ability to size up a situation and know what to pay attention to. In every situation there's noise, and then there's the things that matter, and successful franchisees know what to ignore. So it's *who* to ignore and *who* to pay attention to, and it's *what* to ignore and *what* to pay attention to."

Let's come back to one of the strengths of the franchise business model for a moment. If you're struggling with how to figure out where and how to start implementing KPIs, your franchisor should have a baseline of the most important elements to measure.

Don Elliott, a 57-location franchisee with Great Clips, the world's largest single-brand hair salon franchise system, uses goal setting and KPIs as a strategic baseline: "My daughter and I set the standards in that first salon of what we saw that we could do. From that point going forward, we used those numbers as kind of a baseline as we opened the second, third, fourth, and fifth salon, and so on. We set our expectations higher than what the corporate guidelines really are."

Don also made one of the best defining statements about the importance of KPIs that I have heard in my career: "You get what you tolerate. You've just got to keep pushing and driving. Of course, we knew [our goals were] attainable, as we'd already proven it could be done. So, if I go back to the next manager and say, 'Well, if this person can do it, why can't you? Let's figure it out. We can get it done.' That's the approach we've taken."

TPFs clearly understand and recognize that KPIs are simply micro truths about specific parts of their businesses that inform the progress they are making towards their goals.

GROWTH PLAN EXERCISE 8-2
What do you tolerate?

Don's words are powerful and force us to think about possibility and potential. For this exercise, think about these questions:

- In your day-to-day, what are you willing to tolerate? Premises that could use a boot shine? Less than desirable engagement in your employees? Customer experience that is okay but not great? Inconsistent communication with the franchisor? Mediocrity in your own leadership?

- In your day-to-day, what is not getting done that can make a difference to your revenue, to your customers, and to your team that would raise everyone's spirits and make tomorrow less of a struggle? What if you could have ongoing insight into how well your team is doing at getting the right work done, and progressively tolerate less and less slack, downtime or mistakes?

- What if you could progressively work towards getting your team to operate at or above a more aggressive level of excellence (positive tolerance) in order to meet or exceed your objectives? It could be life-altering for you and your business, couldn't it?

In the Beginning

In an optimum scenario, when opening a new franchise, the franchisee starts by following the franchisor's directions regarding setup, then starts marketing and hiring the right people. If done well, the franchisee trains employees on processes and skills, communicates behavior and activity expectations and goals, and explains how the franchisor's established lead and lag KPIs will be used to ensure optimum performance and achievement of the desired goals. Then, on an ongoing basis, the franchisee communicates progress and results with the team. This develops a healthy culture that enables rapid duplication in order to scale and grow.

When I interviewed Joel Winters in March 2020, he had only been a franchisee with Kitchen Tune-Up (KTU) for two and a half years, and in such a short time he had already become a member of KTU's TPF club, an astounding accomplishment when you consider that KTU has been in business since 1988 and has over 160 franchisees. When I asked Joel what his superpowers were, he said this:

> I really love managing people and helping them grow and succeed. Superpowers are usually related to something that you enjoy doing, and so for me, the managing of people aspect of it is very natural. One of my favorite parts is watching a young person come up and gain new skills and confidence, and then grow as a result of your influence.
>
> A secondary one—data analysis, or really, truly knowing your numbers. It's fairly natural for me to analyze our business and figure out where we have weaknesses and where we have opportunities. That makes me tick, because I know there's always something else that we can do to make our people better, and there's always something else we can do to make our processes more effective.

Unfortunately, optimum scenarios like Joel's rarely happen, because the learning curve for new franchisees is so steep. When they buy a franchise and launch the business, it's like being teleported into a completely new body—and that's exactly what it is, a new "business body" that the franchisee has to become familiar with. It's a demanding learning curve, managed with the franchisor's guidance and direction. The franchisor's systems and processes are the bones, tendons and muscles, and the system-baseline KPI data are the neurotransmitters of pain and pleasure signals of the business's central nervous system. The franchisee must step into the new body and start running. Before they can run, they have to learn a few things first—to crawl, then stand, then walk, and only then start learning how to run.

The challenge is this: so many new franchisees are so focused on "doing the work of the business" and so busy trying to coordinate many different new things in their business body that they aren't taking any time to pay attention to the KPI nerve signals. They just keep putting their head down and believe that by exerting their sheer force of will and blunt-force effort they can ignore the pain signals, hoping they'll eventually go away. This, they think, will be enough to get them through. What they don't realize is that they are developing and embedding behaviors that will handcuff their ability to achieve better results once the business is up and running.

You might be a seasoned entrepreneur or have many years of experience under your belt in your current franchise, but this doesn't mean you've mastered your business body; instead, it might mean that you're only using parts of the business body while you've overlooked unused muscle that continues to atrophy and hold you back. Often, the longer you've been operating your business without using KPIs, or using them minimally, the bigger the challenge will be for you to implement them, because you have to be open to learning a new way of doing things. This is another sign of being stuck in the independence maturity phase I described in the previous chapter.

You have to allow yourself to be more vulnerable while you learn a new way. It's worth repeating Jason Zickerman's words here about people new to franchising: "It's been a long time since they were not good at something. And so that skillset to learn something new, to commit, to becoming excellent, to be willing, to be able to make mistakes that normally you haven't made maybe for years and your earlier career, and be forgiving to a certain point, but committed to becoming better is mission critical."

I'm confident that as you've progressed though this book, you've been able to identify some of the "crawl, then stand, then walk" steps you might have skipped or only taken a cursory glance at when you launched your business that are now preventing you from running well. Now that you've got deeper awareness of the importance of KPIs, I'm betting that the glossing over your franchise's KPI neural network that you may have done in your early days will jump out to you as one of the most evident skipped areas.

GROWTH PLAN EXERCISE 8-3
What might need changing?

Jason Zickerman talks about the need to build a new skillset, to change your way of thinking.

1. On a scale of 1 to 10, how ready are you to be a bit more vulnerable, to be open to an enhanced way of doing things?
2. What would your redefined business look like, if you know you could get there?
3. How would that redefined business impact your personal and family life?
4. What are the most important KPIs that you need to get better at knowing, now?

Take some time to reflect on these questions, as they help build a solid motivational foundation as you encounter the challenges that come with implementing a KPI neural network. Next, go back to the four-zone aware-sense exercise you did in chapter 3 and look at what you determined were your most pressing challenges. Ask yourself, "How can KPI data help my business progress past our current position? What KPI guidance and data do I need from my franchisor to give me better insight into business performance?"

If you can commit to improving your skills in the critical matter of KPI tracking and measuring, once done, incredible results will be within your grasp. By activating the right KPI neural network, the health of your business will radically improve, and you can then grow at the pace and trajectory that you desire.

TOM TAUBE'S GROWTH JOURNEY

Here's a real-life example of someone who did exactly this. Tom Taube started his career as a sales engineer with a Fortune 500 company and stayed with them for six years. He then started his own business and ran it for ten years before selling it to a public company and staying on with the new owners for several more years. So,

Tom is no slouch. He got bitten by the entrepreneurial bug though, and after working with a franchise broker, he bought his Kitchen Tune-Up (KTU) franchise fifteen years ago. Tom was able to run a good KTU business and created a good lifestyle for himself, but he was not among the franchisor's top producers.

Two and a half years ago that all changed when the franchisor implemented a system-wide KPI tracking and measuring system, and Tom Taube was one of the early adopters. For thirteen years, Tom was getting good results. But then, in less than two years after implementing the new KPI system, Tom more than doubled his overall revenues and improved his operational efficiencies and profit percentages. Now that Tom has crystal clarity on his KPIs, he is setting an audacious goal of a 5x increase over the next few years, and he has absolute confidence that he'll achieve it now that he knows the pathways to get there.

So, Tom operated for many years at good levels, but then implemented KPI systems and incredible growth took place, incredibly fast.

Tom wasn't the only franchisee in the KTU system to realize such meteoric growth after a multi-year plateau. Heidi Morrissey, the president of KTU, drove the implementation of KPIs across all of her franchisees system-wide. Here's what she shared about the outcome: "In just the last eighteen to twenty-four months, after putting a performance measurement system in place that franchisees actually use, many franchisees saw sales grow by 200 to 300 percent— even franchisees who had been franchisees for over eighteen years!"

What might be possible for you if you can activate your business neural network and adopt better utilization of your KPI data?

As we shared in chapter 5, which covered leadership, communicating goals and objectives to your team and directing them towards taking hyper-focused action are critical parts of success. This includes measuring that performance and communicating KPI-based progress back to your team; remember that the quality of that communication is only as good as the quality of the KPI data you're using.

Understanding and revisiting your most important KPIs regularly is critical to maintaining current success levels and enabling future growth and opportunity. Whether you're a newer franchisee

or well-tenured, the stronger the KPI data you utilize, the more activated your business neural network becomes, which then drives
greater awareness and aware-sense, as we saw in chapter 3.

Doing nothing new is also one of your choices. If you want to
grow your business and improve your results, but aren't willing to
change anything about how you're gathering and utilizing KPI data,
well, then the definition of insanity might fit. Consider a famous
and relevant quote from George Santayana: "Those that fail to learn
from history are doomed to repeat it."

SURVEY 8-1:
KPIs and Resources

Use this survey to assess which areas of your business would benefit
from implementing or improving Key Performance Indicators.

On a scale of applicability (1 = not applicable to 10 = highly applicable), which of the following KPIs could help you grow your business and solve problems?	Low 1-4	Medium 5-7	High 8-10
• A goal achievement KPI to measure progress in relation to accomplishing our customer experience goals with specifics–not generalities. The desired result is that if we had more concrete ways of measuring progress, we could identify our stuck points and deal with them. For example, if customer satisfaction is not increasing at the rate it should be, the stuck point could be the use of a Net Promoter Score and not using a more robust tool to find out why.			
• A marketing performance KPI that can identify how well we are doing on market outreach. The desired result is to ascertain how our marketing initiatives need to pivot to have a more direct appeal to our primary market. For example, we might be using the wrong social media to reach our market or our messaging might not have the effect we want it to have to drive interest in our products or services.			

On a scale of applicability (1 = not applicable to 10 = highly applicable), which of the following KPIs could help you grow your business and solve problems?	Low 1-4	Medium 5-7	High 8-10
• A goal achievement KPI using specifics, not generalities, to measure progress in accomplishing our sales and business generation goals.			
• A goal achievement KPI using specifics, not generalities, to measure progress in accomplishing our production/fulfillment goals.			
• A set of financial management KPIs that can be aggregated on a one-page dashboard and show me our cash flow position; daily, weekly, and monthly sales; and cost of sales. The desired result is to assess how we are doing on day-to-day operations management.			
Use the remaining lines to insert other KPIs that you're currently using or would like to implement:			
•			
•			
•			
•			
•			
•			

TIP: Reach out to your franchisor. Your franchisor should be able to provide clear direction regarding which KPIs are the most important to pay attention to.

FRANCHISE CEOS uniformly said their top-performing franchisees "know their numbers"; they diligently track and measure their key business performance data. Several CEOs went so far as to say that their TPFs knew their numbers before the franchisor's tracking data got released by head office.

When asked during my interviews what one or two areas of improvement this book must address, most of these same CEOs shared that a large number of their franchisees take far too casual an approach to KPI tracking. This corresponds strongly with my own experience in every franchise system I've ever been directly involved in—and in over thirty years in this industry, I've worked with hundreds of brands. This phenomenon of not tracking KPI is also a rampant problem the vast majority of non-franchised small business owners share.

TPFs track and measure their KPIs and regularly block off time to review the data—weekly, monthly, quarterly or annually. They aren't looking at the data for data's sake or for giving themselves a pat on the back for how well they've done; they are striving to identify what can be gleaned from the data and *learn* from it. They study the relationship between their lead indicators (current activities) and lag indicators (results and outcomes from recent activities), comb through their KPI data, and constantly seek insight into where they can make mid-course adjustments, either to move faster towards capitalizing on opportunity, or to arrest mistakes and reduce undesirable performance in their business.

It cannot be overemphasized how important monitoring KPIs is. Each franchise system has some common KPIs that most businesses share; in addition, they should have some specific KPIs that are unique to their own business model and system.

Please complete the survey and Growth Plan Exercises in this chapter before moving on to the final chapter, in which tilling the soil reveals some truths about franchising.

Driver No. 7 Takeaways
List your top three takeaways from this chapter:

1. _____

2. _____

3. _____

CHAPTER 9

BECOMING UNSTOPPABLE

WHAT IS IT TO BE UNSTOPPABLE? When you do a Google search on the book title "unstoppable," thirty-nine book cover images show up on the first page alone. Some books are about how A-list athletes or celebrities got to the top, some are a collection of inspirational stories, and some are kids' books. My favorite book title of the bunch was *Be Unstoppable: The Art of Never Giving Up*, by Bethany Hamilton. I was attracted to the picture of a surfer on the cover, and the subtitle *The Art of Never Giving Up* speaks to me as an entrepreneur, franchise search coach, business coach, and as an author.

With so many books that provide advice on being unstoppable, you might ask why I would want to pick this word for the title of my own book. My answer is twofold: first, because nothing has been written on the subject for you, the franchise owner; and the far more important second reason is that this book is about helping you write your own "becoming unstoppable" story from this point on in your business and personal life.

If you've had any time at all in the saddle of running your business, it likely speaks to you as well, because is that not the essence of what got you to this point? You're still running your business, correct? Despite all the scrapes, bumps, bruises, trials and tribulations, your reserves of resilience haven't run out yet.

To me, being unstoppable is not about getting to superstardom, becoming an elite athlete, or even a top franchisee. It's far simpler than that. Becoming unstoppable starts with a choice. You're still running your business, so you've already made an important choice somewhere along the line—somehow, some way, you've been living "being unstoppable." It's important that you acknowledge and celebrate that.

But the choice that's in front of you right now, in this moment, is to commit to reaching the next level in your business, to improve something that can incrementally move the needle. Think of it as a "power-up" badge in a video game. You might choose a shield or an additional degree of strength. Each of the seven drivers you have read about will have that power-up effect. Cumulatively, they will have a multiplier, not just an add-on, effect.

In these pages you've heard from many top-performing franchisees and franchisor CEOs who are using the seven drivers every day in their business. In their own words you can see the incredible results that come with doing so.

Start with the Soil

What should your next power-up be? Well, that's not for me to say, because it will be different for every franchise owner. The exercises in this book should be helping you get closer to knowing what that answer is. If you're still struggling, here's a different perspective.

My sister-in-law, Mary, is a novelist and one of my sources of inspiration. During our last visit she was working on her seventh book. We've had numerous conversations about writing. In a recent discussion, I shared that I'm curious about how, from nothing, she can create an entire cast of characters and build a story. She shared this advice that she heard at a book convention: "Start with the soil."

She said that to start the creative process, she starts with thinking about what kind of soil there is where the story is going to take place—is it rich or is it hardscrabble? What kind of crops will it sustain? What kind of people can live off the land? What tools do they need to work the land? What type of community will the land sustain?

This made total sense, and I was fascinated. I began to expand on Mary's metaphor: The farmer has to cut down trees and remove rocks and plow the soil to plant the seeds. That's a lot of hard labor. And it takes a while for the crops to grow. How are the people going to sustain themselves after planting the first crop? These early homesteaders have to bring several months of foodstuffs and other supplies with them while their first plantings germinate and grow. They will work the land, water the plants, and remove nutrient-stealing weeds. They'll hunt and forage to extend their food supplies.

So, how can starting with the soil be relevant to you, the franchise owner?

Mary's metaphor couldn't be more perfect. The very nature of the franchise business model is that you've already bought your "plot of land" that has a moderately rich soil; you've already been working this field of opportunity for a while. Many of the rocks, tree stumps, and roots have been cleared because the franchisor has already prepped your ground, and the ground of your peer franchisees. The community to support you—suppliers and vendors, peer franchisees, the franchisor support team—has already been built and is thriving.

The franchisor has taught you how to work the land, and has even given you the fertilizer (marketing strategies and sales methodologies); they've also advised you what machinery to buy, and trained you how to plant, water, weed, and harvest.

Like any farmer, you've just got to get out in the field you've chosen and work the land. The fertilizer has to be put into the ground, and the seeds have to get sown—every season. And when you do things right, some seasons you'll get a bumper crop. Other seasons, not as much, but every successful farmer is 100 percent committed to working the land, from planting to harvesting, and much else in between. Every season.

GROWTH PLAN EXERCISE 9-1
How well are you working your soil?

Reflect for a moment on how well you've been working the field of opportunity that is your franchise:

- How well have you worked the land up until now? What kind of crop have you been nurturing and growing?
- Have you been producing a crop that's rich and abundant, or one that's meager and barely enough to survive on?
- How well have you followed your franchisor's guidance and utilized the tools available to maximize the opportunity?

Think for a moment about the point you're currently at in your franchise ownership journey. Regardless of how little or how much success you've enjoyed up until now, look at this point through the farmer's eyes. It's the beginning of the new season, and you're preparing to start the season's work. What are the lessons from your previous seasons that you can start applying now? Which components of this book speak to you the loudest, that you'll want and need to pay attention to as you start to plan out how you're going to execute this season's work?

Now take it up a notch. Instead of just thinking about the start of this season, reflect on what you want the results to be at its end. What are your goals for the coming year?

At some point in the past you gave yourself an incredible gift of freedom, of self-accountability, and of self-responsibility. That gift carries a lot of weight, doesn't it? You bought a franchise with proven systems and processes that enable you to have the autonomy and freedom to make operational and financial decisions, and the flexibility to choose how and when to make those decisions. Even if not all of the systems are perfect (they rarely are), and even if the model has evolved into something different than you expected (and every franchise system does evolve), you still have the freedom to choose what actions to take, or to choose more inaction.

As you've learned from the many voices that contributed to this book, there's always more room to grow. What might that growth look like for you?

Start with the soil ...

Write Your Own Unstoppable Story

Here's what Gary Findley, CEO of Restoration 1, says about his top franchisees knowing "the theme of their story": "I think it's their personal vision, and I think it's a personal mission of what they want to accomplish... And then they all have an end goal and they ask 'How do I get there? How long does it take me to get there?' That end goal could be to build a business and sell it. It could be to build a business for ten years. It could be to keep doing it until they retire. It could be build a business to turn it over to a family member. Whatever that goal is, they all seem to know what it is."

Becoming unstoppable is not someone else's journey or story—it is yours. As you step into the next season of your business, what revisions to your story do you want to make? Maybe you want to write an entirely new story. How can you make your story become a reality, and a reality that's more aligned with your purpose and values? You've learned the seven drivers of next-level growth that are ubiquitous across all franchise sectors, and I've provided you with a robust set of Growth Plan Exercises to help foster your creative thinking and narrow your focus to which driver will have the most impact, now. All that's left is for you to take a next-level action on something, somewhere in your business. So as you prepare to embark on that journey, grab a comfortable chair and a refreshing beverage, and reflect on the tips that follow, which are a collage of quotes from some of our industry's most successful franchisees and CEOs of franchise systems. Pay attention to what quotes stick with you, as those ideas may be catalysts to help you launch the next leg of your franchise ownership journey.

Tips on Next-Level Growth from Those Who Have Gone Before

We have reached the point in the book where the author makes the great reveal. The one recipe that can satisfy all tastes. In this case, how all of the drivers work in harmony to provide you, the franchise owner, with the knowledge and tools to scale your business, in a box neatly tied with a bow.

To suggest this can be done is disingenuous. As you have patiently read the book and reflected on your progress to date, and have been thinking about your challenges and opportunities, you know just how complex your business is. As Colin Bates said, "I find in this business it is never one shot and done. It's never a silver bullet where you go, 'Oh, I figured out the end game. I've got it now. If I just do this one thing, everything is going to be great.' Business doesn't work that way. You try something and it may or may not work. If you fail, you try again. Try something a little bit differently, but never give up." Within these words, Colin has captured the very essence of becoming unstoppable.

That's a great tip, and it inspired me to think that you would prefer to hear from our extraordinary collective brain trust on ideas, processes, and action steps of top-performing franchisees that can empower you to become unstoppable yourself. These are in no particular order or ranking, because some tips will have more relevance for one franchisee over another. Some of these tips appear for a second time because they are a great match with the themes in this section.

PURPOSE

"At the end of the day, everybody that's going to be in our business has to have a purpose. My purpose is two major things. I've got three young kids that I've got to set a great example for so they can be stewards of this country and make a positive impact. And then, more importantly, if I have the ability to build and scale businesses and make an impact on people to live the American dream through business ownership, why wouldn't I do that?"—JOSH SKOLNICK

"I definitely think that there has to be some level of passion or desire to be able to run the business the way that they want to. So if they're not in it wholeheartedly, they're not going to have the best results. It's like that person that is negative all the time. If they're getting in it and they're just wanting to make money off of it, and they're coming in with only one train of thought, it's probably not going to be an overall win."—EMILY WILCOX

"Top performers are purpose driven. They understand the purpose and they drive with purpose. It's really important that good franchisees understand more than just the financial metrics. They understand the vision and the purpose of what they're doing. There's a greater good to what they're doing typically when they're in those top performers. They're just very purpose driven on something that is greater than the execution of how to generate dollars for the business."—DAVE MORTENSEN

"I think that our franchisees that perform at the highest level are franchisees that are very purposeful about what they do. They're 100 percent committed to their businesses and their people. And they have a level of passion and commitment to what they're doing and just a connection to everyone in their business to bring it forward and make it successful."—NED LYERLY

HAPPINESS

"The foundation is you have to love the business you choose to get into. It's just like I tell my kids—you need to pick a career that you're going to love doing, because if you don't love it, what's the point? We have one life to live. It's just like a business. If you're not into dry cleaning, if that doesn't inspire you, then I wouldn't recommend it. You have to really love what you're doing, because if you don't, you're just going to be mediocre. You have to love what you do, because it will show."—HEATHER STANKARD

"I find the happiest people are the ones that make a decision that they are responsible for their happiness. And the things that I do to keep myself happy are that I fill my mind with positive quotes. I work on having gratitude. I keep a gratitude journal. I make sure I exercise, because that's good for my health, and good health helps you maintain a good outlook. And I make sure I eat whole food, unprocessed food, because all of that works together. Most importantly, I believe it's the decision to develop and maintain a positive mindset and a growth mindset.

"To me it's all about the importance of culture and being an employer of choice. Even if you're a small single-unit franchise, make your people feel loved and appreciated and manage the KPIs." —CATHERINE MONSON

"[Our top franchisees] have a deep sense of ownership in the brand. They're not using our brand. They make the brand their own, and they're in love with it because it's their brand. And they're the first ones to step up and speak for the brand, defend the brand, enhance the brand, protect the brand. You know, ultimately it comes down to this: you want to build ownership in your franchisees, and when they build ownership, they become connected, and they're the happiest because they understand there's no perfect world out there. We have to get up every day, open our eyes and go fight the battle in order to grow our businesses. And those are the ones who are proud of wearing the jersey that they're wearing on their team. They're not just there to make a buck. They're there to make a difference." —ADAM CONTOS

"Our business is very important to us all, but it cannot be all we have, because I think that hurts your ability to ride the tide, the ups and the downs. With balance in your life, it helps keep everything in perspective.

"And I think when you have no balance in your life, then things become catastrophic that otherwise would be, 'Oh, well. That's something I can deal with tomorrow.' I also think that happy people are those with relationships outside their office, within the franchise and other positive people. If you want to be happy, you surround yourself with other positive, happy people. If you want to be miserable, pick out all the Debbie Downers and plug into them. We are who we associate with. So the happy people I see are the ones with the good support system of other happy, productive, motivated people and they feed off each other." —JANIA BAILEY

"Those that have a clear vision seem to be most content and happy. It's those that are always trying to figure out and readjust, and don't quite know what they want out of life or what they want out of this small business, who are not as happy. The happy ones are results driven, and they do it each and every day."—DOUG BRAUER

"Happy people are really the easiest people to manage as long as they feel like they're part of something that's meaningful, and you engage them and you give them opportunities, not only to help themselves, but to help others. I know so many people that I've worked with that are franchisees have just loved the fact that we respect them enough to ask and they love that. That just really floats their boat."—KEITH GERSON

TEAM

"If you're going to be successful—I don't care what franchise you're running—if you don't have a great team behind you, you're not going to be successful. There's no way.

"How do you build the team? Through time, hiring the right people, interviewing, and finding out what their goals are and if they're going to be a good fit for your team."—DOUG BRAUER

"Building a fantastic team is very important, and you can't do this all on your own. Invest in people in terms of paying them well, rewarding them well, compensating them through bonuses, profit sharing. We have people who've been with us ten-plus years and have grown with the company. Team is very important to me. Invest in the team. Working on the business in the business is very important. Think about how to grow the business versus thinking about how to get a product out of the door."—SAROSH NAYAR

"The happiest franchisees in the top 4 percent are TEAM (Together-Everyone-Achieves-More) players, and we know there is no 'I' in team. They have the respect and admiration of their management and staff. They are cooperative and friendly with their peers."—JOHN PRITTIE

"The top performers are people who understand team. They are people who invest in their business. They don't just invest financially. Everybody does that when they start, but you keep investing. You reinvest in that business. And more importantly, you invest in relationships with your team in your local marketplace, with key customer groups and people groups like that."—STEVE WHITE

INNOVATION

"With Jan-Pro, you have the ability to work within the framework that's provided to you to make it better. I would encourage franchise owners and franchisees to look at what they bring to the table that could make the business better. If that's not your core strength, then listen to others that have done that. Don't be afraid to try it in your own organization."—COLIN BATES

"How do you establish that mindset of, how do I innovate? How do I go that extra mile to help the customer? I think it yields results in the long term. And for a lot of my customers right now, we are that marketing consultancy company. And it's the solutions that they come to us for that transcend what people think of as regular signage company."—SAROSH NAYAR

"Every part of our strategic vision is to go, 'Okay, how are we going to best work with our leading performers to execute on the future of where this brand can go?' They're a very large part of the innovation work that is going on in the business at all times. Call them the innovators of the business, both from an execution level and thoughtful ideas as well, because they're the ones that are going to give your best ideas. So, you're going to have to make sure you're always listening to your franchisees and giving them a place to be able to be heard."—DAVE MORTENSEN

"As a franchisor, we have the intellectual property. We create a lot of innovation and tools and systems. But the [top performers] also can create and add value, and we've learned a lot from them over the years. And they've added a lot to the franchise system as well. And they've been extremely entrepreneurial from the early days in building this brand, and they're great valued partners with us and the franchise community as a whole."—NED LYERLY

"All models are innovating today. They're getting more customer focused, and that involves change. And so if a franchisee continues to learn and be very agile along with their franchisor, I think they're going to be positioned for success. [Franchisees] tend to be lifelong learners."—GRAHAM WEIHMILLER

RELATIONSHIPS

"Our goal has always been to do the most that we can for our unit franchisees. That's really been the driver from day one. Our business is so special, so neat, because the more we're able to selflessly give for the benefit of others—our units—the more successful we are. It's something I try to teach my kids and try to apply to my relationship with my wife, because I found that to be true in every aspect of my life. And the great thing is we get to apply that principle here at work every single day.

"There are four pillars that Jack and Carol [the franchisor] told us when we bought the business that we needed to focus on every day. And I think to this day when I go home, this is how I do a self-audit on whether or not my day was productive, because we don't sell a franchise every day. We don't sign an account every day. So... how do I determine if I made a difference? Did I have a positive impact in the four things within the Jan-Pro model? I have to touch—every single day as owner of the business—something that has an impact on my account sales, something that has an impact on franchise sales, something that has an impact on receivables and something that has an impact on my account retention. So, I think those offices that are mired in mediocrity, they don't touch those four things every single day."—BRAD RUSH

"[Good relationships are founded on] the ability to engender trust and commitment in others. So trust is where people feel safe dealing with you. They don't feel you are going to kind of give it to them in the back or do something that could hurt them. And commitment is the ability to motivate other people into action. It's the ability to influence others and build trust and commitment.

"Sometimes people feel betrayed later on [in their tenure with their franchisor]...A franchisee said to me once, 'He treated me like royalty to start with. Now he treats me like royalties,' but successful people are able to sustain that relationship of trust long term."– GREG NATHAN

"You've got to be able to relate to people. You've got to be able to talk to them, understand them and listen to them. You've actually got to hear them. You've got to respond to what they're looking for. I think the magic is to understand the why in why they do what they do.

"You think, 'What are these people doing?' If you get inside their head, and you really understand what their world is like, and what their perspective is, you can help coach them through that. That, to me, is magical for these folks, and probably in every organization.

"Being able to coach them, set high expectations, hold them accountable, and then executing are really the other things that I think about when I look at top traits."–DON ELLIOTT

"The franchisees are out there 'owning the community.' We live in a world based on relationships. If you do not know how to build relationships, you will never get to that superior level."–JOSH YORK

"Being in this business for twenty-five years now, and having the customers I do have, they've become more than customers. They've become friends. It's not always about the sale. The sale will always come. Build a relationship with the customer.

"We're not curing cancer here. We're making signs and graphics for people. And I always tell my staff, 'These are people, just like you and me. They're our friends. They're our neighbors. They're part of our community, and community involvement is good. So just remember that. We're just people working with other people.'"– DOUG BRAUER

VALUES

"I think my business is really about me. You know, it's an extension of my personality—how I run it says a lot about me personally. It speaks to my own personal value system, [and] high on that list are kindness, hard work, and integrity. So everything that I do in my business should reflect that. I want to be proud of my business. I want to have relationships with people that are based on those things. And I choose vendors, employees and clients that share those same kinds of values."—CYNTHIA KEENAN

"All my core values really align with my business model. It's about being authentic. My number one thing is I value people first as opposed to the bottom line, and I know that sounds counterproductive. But for me, that really works. I value both my team and my clients.

"I'm always looking for ways to help our community and that help get our brand awareness out there as well. So it helps me meet my core values and also helps us build the business, and it helps our community so we're all served well."—HEATHER STANKARD

"We're able to set big goals because I know my core values. It's who I am. I have clarity around that. I can set goals as big as the moon and it doesn't scare me, because at the end of the day I'm going to live and die by my values and my convictions, for who I am, what I stand for, and what I'm willing to live and die for."—ANGELA BROWN

AWARENESS

"If all we do is talk and we don't act upon the things that we talk about, we have no credibility as a leader. You're just a figurehead, and that's not going to lead to positive results. I think I'm constantly aware of what I'm projecting. I think the ability to be empathetic to other people is a great sign of awareness that is often overlooked. I think EQ is probably a greater predictor of success than IQ. I think most successful people are probably self-aware, and even those who are narcissistic in nature are probably aware of it. And that might drive tremendous success. But their definition of success is defined differently than what mine is."—BRAD RUSH

"It is very important to develop and heighten that sense of awareness, that acuteness of what's going on in the business, what's going on in the community. It's all interrelated. You can't just open a business and say, 'Hey, that's all I want to do.' If you want to be successful, you've got to be connected to the world around you. Have your finger on the pulse of different things. We've got to do that so many different ways as somebody in a small business. We're on several committees. We do volunteering work. We get known and we take in information from other folks from all walks of life. And I think that just forms a complete person. I think that it helps you form a more solid, robust business."—SAROSH NAYAR

RESILIENCE

"Resilience obviously is a really important one. It's especially important for entrepreneurship. Because with entrepreneurs, you're failing over and over again.

"There are things you can do to build your resilience muscle. First of all, having self-awareness if your resilience is low, and there are different psychometric profiles you can take to measure resilience. But knowing that about yourself is important, because you want to focus on building that muscle."—DAN MONAGHAN

"The number one trait [of top performers] is resilience: Things are going to come at you no matter what."—HEIDI MORRISSEY

"Failure is a very important component to success. I have a PhD in failing. I have a master's degree in getting back up. I never quit. You have a better chance of seeing elephants fly than seeing me quit."—JOSH YORK

"[In] any franchise, you've got good months and you've got bad months. You've got peaks and you've got valleys. And without resiliency, you can't survive those downward turns; you can't see the upward turn that's coming.

"People with resiliency bounce back from setbacks and they don't let those setbacks define them. They're looking for 'How do I work through, around, over, under, and get through this?' And people without that kind of resiliency have the tendency to just throw up their hands and quit. They only see the negative. So for me, that's probably the number one trait anyone going into any shape, form, or fashion of business needs to have."—JANIA BAILEY

ENGAGEMENT

"I think there are two things there. One is being engaged in your business on a regular, periodic basis if you're not [the on-site] owner-operator. And then the other thing is engaging with your community. That's your community of guests, but it's also your community out there in your neighborhood, so that you can develop those opportunities for collaborations, cross-promotions, referrals, all that networking that helps drive traffic to your business."—VANESSA YAKOBSON

"Top performers are also very engaged in thinking about the system more as a whole piece that we can all contribute to, and not just as, 'my little piece over here.' When you become very self-centered, very locked into your area, you tend to kind of lose focus that there is a lot of us doing very similar things. So, be engaged and helpful."—HEIDI MORRISSEY

COMPASSION

"Pride and compassion come into play as top performers deliver service to their customers, and you can watch their unit franchisees succeed. These are not initial motivational drivers, but they become important quickly in a way that is very different from their financial success."—JACK LAPOINTE

"We always say there are two ingredients that make a good franchisee. One is a caring heart—people that have the right heart for the business who want to care for others; they want to give back to their communities. The other side is good business skills, being able to hire the right people, finding the right talent, finding people with compassionate hearts that also want to be involved in a community-based caring business."—LANE KOFOED

"Really good leaders are really good at unlocking motivations for human intent, and to be able to do that, you have to have a compassion for who they are, what they're about, what were their key drivers to be where they are today and what are their key drivers and motivators for the future.

"What I have found with human intent is that everyone is unique. So it's like understanding a snowflake and if you know anything about a snowflake, no two flakes are alike. If you understand that every individual is like a snowflake, and you take the time and have the curiosity to find out what their intentions and motivators are, you can put the things in front of them that are going to drive the best performance for them."—DAVE MORTENSEN

"Caring and kindness. Leaders truly care about the people in their organization and the staff in their offices. They see the role as leading and helping people, not managing the bottom line."—ADAM CONTOS

SERVICE

"You must delight your customers. Part of it is being innovative, the ability to delight your customers at every touch point. It starts with the attitude, how you pick up the phone and how you talk to customers, and the delivery of the products on time, meeting and exceeding all of the customer's requirements. And that leads to having long-term customers and repeat business."—SAROSH NAYAR

"Understand and deliver a great experience to the customer. How you interact with a customer, and the response and reaction from that customer, is incredibly important, because they will tell others and be your repeat business."—DOUG PHILLIP

"Solution selling. To do that, you have to listen, you have to find out what the customer wants, and then you have to solve any problems that arise. Gather all the facts and then develop the solution. And you have to be able to communicate that solution to the customer, and explain it so they understand why and what you're doing, and why it's a better choice than something else."—TOM TAUBE

TRAINING

"Top performers are spending more time working with their employees, training and supporting them, and nurturing them, and therefore keeping them longer, and getting better results from them."—JOHN PRITTIE

"I think the big thing in any growing business is being able to develop a structure within the business. You're obviously still in charge, and you're leading everything, but you need to develop management, especially if it's people-oriented. And you need to develop good customer service people. And empowering those people, and training those people to make good decisions when you're not around."—ROB WEDDLE

"As the leader, you've got to help your team tap into what their motivations are. They're not necessarily going to be excited about selling that extra bottle of product or that extra service, unless they're relating it back to their own personal goals and ambitions. Give them the coaching and tools that they need to be successful.

"Know how to say, 'I'm here for you—what do you need from me? What tools can I provide to you? What coaching can I give you? What incentives can I put in place that are going to motivate and inspire you?' And then 'How are we going to work together over time?' Because it's not a one-and-done. It's not a 'Well, I had a staff meeting last month, and they're still not selling?' Someone said to me that the coach is always in training with their athletes. You don't just coach and go away and send them out into the field."—VANESSA YAKOBSON

CULTURE

"When you have a rock-solid foundation culturally first, you can build any successful company, and the reverse could be true. You could have the best widget, the best idea, but if you build it with the wrong people, with the wrong culture, it's going to crumble at some point. I think that the true measure of success is the culture. The more the right people that come on, the more it galvanizes."—STEVE THOMPSON

"It's all about the culture. Our culture is very simple. It's servant leadership, it's accountability, and it's active collaboration. And those three build on each other. Everybody in franchise land wants active-collaboration relationships, where the franchisee and the franchisor work hand-in-hand together. But in my world, I need it because of the huge insurance companies that I serve. But I maintain that no franchisee is willing to enter an active-collaboration relationship with their franchisor unless they first know that that franchisor puts the franchisee's welfare ahead of their own, and is a true servant leader.

"And I say we lead boldly, but with the heart of a servant. So we don't abdicate our leadership responsibilities. We're not here as a vendor. We're always trying to put the franchisee's welfare first, knowing that the long-term view of making a lot of our franchisees really successful, it's going to be an inescapable conclusion that we become a successful franchisor."—STEVE WHITE

"Success is largely [due to] the fact that we've put the right people in the right business, who have followed the system, and we are not at liberty to take any of the credit for the success that they've attained within our systems, because it's truly the culture that's developed the individuals that are in the system—the way they network with each other, the transparency that each franchisee has with each other and the competitive nature we create through the way that we are open and transparent with performance of franchisees."—JOSH SKOLNICK

"It's those top sixteen customers—my team. My opportunity to be a positive influence in their lives, that's number one. I have a philosophy: I want every single team member to look forward to pulling into the parking lot on Monday mornings. So, not just, 'Hey, I like going to work.' But looking forward to it, specifically Mondays, because that's the day when no one wants the weekend to end. And so, my motivation is to create that environment that people want to stay in."—MICHAEL GILPIN

"You need to infuse a high-performance culture throughout your organization, not just inside your corporate office, but throughout your whole franchise system. Culture is more than just a feeling. It's actually a verb, and it's an action. You have to deliver that on a high level. How we do it is really through the four P's. It's a delivery of development of people, both on a personal and a professional level. It'd be driving with your purpose, making sure you have a focus on your profits or performance... Last, but not least, our fourth key would be play. Play is, in essence, bringing levity to your business, but it also brings curiosity. It brings collaboration. It brings communication. Having that element of play always sounds so fluffy, but people call us to say, 'How do we execute on that?'"—DAVE MORTENSEN

VISION
"For a business owner, the single greatest driver of why someone does something, or someone doesn't do something, is their ability to connect with their personal vision of what success is for them. And if they could see that this business or their activity is a clear path to supporting their personal vision of success, whatever that might be, they'll be a top performer, because the motivation is way more than just a bottom-line number of a business. So that's kind of the big difference.

"When your efforts have the ability to reach beyond just the bottom line of the company and make a difference for you and your family, that's the driver, for all privately held business owners regardless, that's really the key to it."—JASON ZICKERMAN

"This isn't about cutting hair. This is about people. This is about being the visionary. I fit that role perfectly. Hate detail and all the shiny stuff. I have great ideas and now have a leadership team that I can count on [to implement them]."—CLARA OSTERHAGE

"The first trait I identified about top franchisees is that they always seem to have a clear vision of where they want to go and they're able to make decisions about what they need to do to get there. Understanding where you want to go is incredibly vital to any business, and this group [of top-performing franchisees] really seems to clearly have a vision of what they want to do and how they want to get there. And if they hit snags along the way, they're able to make the decisions to pivot and keep that journey moving."—DOUG PHILLIP

"We've done lots of franchisee interviews, and there's certain interviews that stick out in my mind. I remember talking to this very successful franchisee who said when he started his business he built out the entire infrastructure of what his business would look like. So he had a clear vision of what all the roles and responsibilities were. The plan was what helped him stay growth-oriented, knowing that at some point he would have to put someone in each of these roles. So, he had an org chart of his future organization from day one."—EDITH WISEMAN

"I'd say of the top performers it's got to be less than 10 or 20 percent of them who came here without quitting a job. They had a vision. They actually had a goal to start their own business. And they gave up something else that was also lucrative to go down this path. The franchisees that come here as a last resort? I call them the 'reluctant entrepreneur.' They might do well, but you have to convince them a little bit more. Whereas the top group, they've thought this through. This is a decision they made. They want to be a business owner, and they have a goal, and they want a plan. They enjoy being educated on franchising. They like the idea of systems. Those are the people that stand the greatest chance to succeed, and I think tend to

be the ones that become your disciples within your system."—ROB
WEDDLE

ADAPTABILITY

"If you don't have that positive attitude and aren't constantly looking for how to make things better, I don't think you can survive in
business. And that leads into the willingness to change. We know if
we're not changing and growing, we're dying in business. You cannot stand still. You must be open to change and trying new things."—
JANIA BAILEY

"Being relentless is important, but pivoting is even more important.
Pivoting is a very, very important thing. You have to innovate, you
have to change. You have to be able to adapt."—JOSH YORK

"[Top performers] believe in and execute the system. If they disagree
with something, they either get over it quickly and we never hear
about it, or they engage with us to make things better. They're positive and energetic. They don't let things get them down. They adapt,
they improvise and they overcome—kind of like the Marines."—ROB
GOGGINS

"Franchisees that are going to be very successful in business will
adapt and pivot and change with the times and reinvest in the business. Those who think that the way that they do business today is
the way they're going to do business for the next ten years, they're
going to die. They are going to fall victim to what I like to call the
slow death."—JOSH SKOLNICK

"I would also say adaptability and flexibility are important traits.
This one, again, it can be trained, but it's a lot easier if you're recruit-
ing someone [a new franchisee] who already is [adaptable] and has
a behavioral background of being an effective leader and an effective communicator. I wish that more franchisees were great team
players."—KEITH GERSON

PLANNING AND EXECUTION

"There's no excuses. And if you have a plan B, you're done. There's no plan B. There's only plan A. People with backup plans just end up backing up and crashing into the wall. You have to be able to execute. And the problem is a lot of people have issues executing because they have backup plans."—JOSH YORK

"Figure out the barriers that are preventing you from achieving the success you want to achieve. Recognize which of those are internal and which are external. Brainstorm about the resources available to you, within our system, outside of our system, and come up with a plan for how you're going to tap into those. And start thinking about goal setting. And maybe get a business coach to help you be accountable, or another franchise partner and set up a peer group."—VANESSA YAKOBSON

"The folks in our organization that are the most positive tend to be very goal oriented and very driven.

"I think a lot about their intentionality. They really plan their work, and they work their plan. Every day they have their lists, and they're getting it done. And it's just that constant kind of intentionality that seems to yield the results. Just like in any business, or business model, I think the most successful franchisees don't become that way overnight. It's either years, or decades, in the making. And so we try to recognize that with our highest-performing franchisees. It didn't happen yesterday; it didn't happen last month. It happened over the last ten years or longer."—GRAHAM WEIHMILLER

"I think the one unique thing that most franchise systems don't do enough of is this: they don't do enough stakeholder mapping. What I mean by that is, imagine going to Thanksgiving dinner and every person sitting at the table is a stakeholder in your business. Who are your stakeholders? It could be your customers. Could be your vendors or your vendor partners. Could be your employees. Could be your shareholders.

"So, think of all the touch points throughout your network. It could be a supplier versus a vendor. It could be a service provider. It could be an outside consultant, whatever those stakeholders are. Then think about doing a stakeholder map, so as you make decisions, you understand who all of those stakeholders are. How does each one of these stakeholders benefit? If you find one that's not going to win, you might have to change the way you're going about your decision-making.

"When you start to think about everybody, what you tend to evolve in your strategy planning will be something really strong because then you can uniquely communicate to each stakeholder how there's intrinsic value for them and what you're trying to accomplish."—DAVE MORTENSEN

"Everything starts with your business plan. And every year we set out with a new business plan where I have my sales goals, and my top-line goal, and I divide it among my sales folks. And then we delve down into how we will meet those goals. What are the areas of opportunity? Where do we need to pivot? All of that becomes part of what we focus on over the next few years, which is part of our yearly planning process."—SAROSH NAYAR

TECHNOLOGY

"People are looking at vastly new technologies today that they didn't even contemplate having to pay for, or even look at, say, two years ago. So it's a rapidly changing dynamic, and franchisees have to be open and flexible to the fact that these things need to be considered. So what I hear very frequently is that the franchisors are trying to accelerate technology adoption, but there's resistance from franchisees, because this is the way we've done it. Not all franchisees. Some are more progressive and might have a technology background, or just find that part of the business very interesting, and so they dig in."—EDITH WISEMAN

"Invest in the right technology and machinery and tools that can make you more efficient and grow your business, and that can allow you to introduce new products and services to your customers profitably. So, right up front, that was the mindset going into the business—I will forgo short-term profits for a longer-term investment."—SAROSH NAYAR

"We always say to people it's not a matter of if technology is going to take over your industry—it's a matter of when. So we work in conjunction and unison with our franchisees [to stay on top of technological advancements]."—JOSH SKOLNICK

"FranConnect is technology for franchisors and their franchisees. And one of the trends that I'm seeing is really more of a reliance [on technology]. There's so many things that can be done with technology that can free people up. A lot of the stuff that we have is designed, for example, operationally, to help people ensure that execution is occurring consistently, that there's playbooks that are available that are helpful in making franchise business consultants effective regardless of their time in their business, because it's leveraging expert systems and it's identifying shortfalls and performance, so people could concentrate on the 20 percent that really create the 80 percent of their success."—KEITH GERSON

THE

GROWTH

HELIX

INTRODUCING
THE GROWTH HELIX

I BRIEFLY MENTIONED the concept of the Growth Helix in the introduction of this book; in this second part, I provide you with in-depth exercises that will enable you to delve deeper into your biggest opportunities and challenges to understand, identify, and build an execution plan to help you accelerate to your next level. You will note that some excerpts in Part Two are duplications of the content from each of the corresponding seven driver chapters. This is intentional, both from the perspective of saving you the effort of going back and forth in the book, and to drive stronger retention based on current adult learning principles.

The Growth Helix is an entirely new model of looking at how highly successful franchisees scale their business. This model is unique to the franchise industry because the core of the Growth Helix is the base operating methodology of the franchisor, also known as "the system," and works like this: the franchisee learns and masters the basics of the system, and builds sustainability by executing those basics as prescribed, while experimenting around the edges, succeeding at some things and failing at others, but constantly seeking the lessons of either, and improving incrementally until they're ready to get to the next level. Then they climb to the next level, and repeat this pattern, then escalate to the next level,

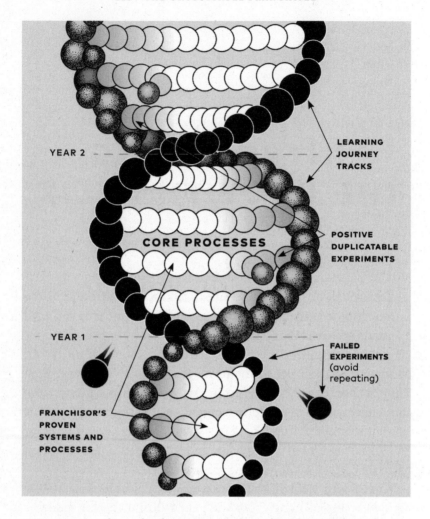

repeat again, then climb again—you get the idea. With each new level comes more opportunity and more desired results.

Situation: Franchisee wants to take their business to the next level, and then the next. In other words, continuously evolve and improve the business, and maybe buy more franchises.

Challenge: The franchisee is stuck and it could be because of one or more of the following: they have operational issues; they need to convert more prospects into customers; they need to improve customer experience and grow customer loyalty; they are suffering a lack of leadership skills and are failing staff in terms of growing them and graduating them into roles with higher accountability; they need to get tighter control of costs.

Solution: The Growth Helix is a graphic representation of mind-set growth and business growth, achieved by overcoming a series of challenges to continuous improvement.

- The center column of this image represents the core systems and processes of the franchise model you bought into. Sticking with the processes and working with the franchisor to make improvements are essential to operating a successful franchise.

- The outer rings represent the learning journey, or experimenting around the edges of the core. The light ring represents those incremental changes that make a positive change to efficiencies and productivity, and the dark ring represents changes that do not improve the business.

Executing the "core" track well ensures you maintain and protect your current levels of performance, while at the same time putting some resources (time, energy, some money if necessary) into the "experimenting" track enables you to explore ways to optimize the business to evolve to your next performance level.

1. Core track: This is doing what you know works, every day, every week, every month. It's following the franchisor's business model and executing the core elements to the best of your ability. It's what "got you to here."

2. Experimental track: This is what you do once your core track is running smoothly. It's trying new things; it's being curious and testing the boundaries of some elements of your core processes to see if there are new, or different, ways to get better results. A key part of experimenting is keeping detailed notes of the experiments and measuring results.

Using the following table will enable you to conduct what is called a risk experiment whenever you're considering changing some element of your business systems. Take a process you use that is core to your business. You know your numbers such as cost of goods and labor. How might results change based on changing suppliers? Will quality remain consistent? Impact on delivery times? New production problems that consume staff time and therefore increase labor costs?

As stated above, this is all about being curious and testing the boundaries of some elements of your core processes to see if there are new, or different, ways to get better results. Remember to keep detailed notes of the experiment and its results, and measure the operational and financial impact of the experiment to see if the new activity is worth repeating and permanently implementing, or rejecting and sticking with the core process.

TABLE A-1: COSTS VS. RESULTS

Experimentation Cost vs. Core Track (Existing) Process	Better Result	Identical Result	Lower Result
NAME OF PROCESS			
Higher cost			
Identical cost			
Lower cost			

	More	Identical	Fewer
Labor hours			
Machine/technology hours			

Can new process be easily duplicated?   Yes ___ / No ___

Can new process be easily taught?   Yes ___ / No ___

Navigating Your Growth Helix

Let's accept that growth is an ongoing journey throughout our lives. The more purposeful and intentional we are about managing our growth, the more robust the experience and results will be. The Growth Helix is a visual representation of this upward-spiral growth journey. This journey is applicable whether you're running a one-person franchise, a single-unit franchise, a multi-unit franchise, or a complex multi-unit/multi-brand enterprise. The variable will be the speed and scale of the journey, and the number of people involved in driving and managing it.

This is also true for franchisors, the primary difference being that franchisees experience the journey first-person and in real time, while franchisors experience much of the journey and experimentation with and through their franchisees. Franchisors who progress intentionally through this journey, and do so with an innovative mindset, achieve their desired outcomes much faster than franchisors who are less aware of the unique interdependence dynamic that great franchise systems possess. (Refer to chapter 7 on interdependence.)

Regardless of which type of franchise business you're involved in running, I invite you to think about and apply the six-step process outlined below as a way to manage your growth and make incremental improvements to your leadership and management skills.

Each of the seven drivers in Part One is linked to the Growth Helix. The order in which you take on each track depends to a degree on your business and how you have prioritized opportunities and challenges. This can be done by a SWOT analysis (strengths, weaknesses, opportunities, threats).

Current and future growth and success are linked to how well you follow the franchisor's system and pay attention to the numbers. Running a successful franchise requires a degree of mastery of the system's operations and an ability to lead. Within two years of buying their franchise, most franchisees have achieved a grasp of the basics. The growth of a business requires ongoing and deliberate practice.

STEP 1: ASSESS THE STRENGTH OF YOUR CURRENT CORE

The first step is to create a baseline reading of business performance, helping you to see how you are meeting or failing to meet your targets and goals. Consider the franchisor's system and operating manual; what operations do you and your team assess as:

- operating at a high level
- operating at a moderate level
- operating at a minimal and unacceptable level

You should engage your staff to give you feedback on how the business is doing. (See chapter 5 for more on employee relationships.) Strive to come up with an objective assessment that acknowledges strengths and weaknesses for you personally, for the operational components of your business, and for your people. What are you and your team:

- executing brilliantly, that you might be able to immediately leverage?
- executing well enough, but where gaps exist that cause occasional issues?
- executing poorly, that are regular sources of frustration and concern?

STEP 2: IDENTIFY POSSIBLE GROWTH AREAS

Growth can occur by taking action to fix problems and by seeing and acting on opportunity.

Use this exercise to identify your most pressing four to six pain points, and then identify your four to six short- and long-term opportunities.

List the Pain Points:

1. _____
2. _____
3. _____
4. _____
5. _____
6. _____

List the Opportunities:

1. _____
2. _____
3. _____
4. _____
5. _____
6. _____

On a scale of 1 (low impact) to 5 (high impact), rate the pain points you have listed:

List and Rate the Pain Points	1	2	3	4	5
1.					
2.					
3.					
4.					
5.					
6.					

Next, order the pain points as you ranked them and describe the steps you can take (or entrust someone to take) to break the challenge into manageable and solvable steps.

Pain Point #1
The actions I will take and by when:

1. _____
2. _____
3. _____

Pain Point #2
The actions I will take and by when:

1. _____
2. _____
3. _____

Pain Point #3
The actions I will take and by when:

1. _____
2. _____
3. _____

Pain Point #4
The actions I will take and by when:

1. _____
2. _____
3. _____

Pain Point #5
The actions I will take and by when:

1. _____
2. _____
3. _____

Pain Point #6
The actions I will take and by when:

1. _____
2. _____
3. _____

On a scale of 1 (low impact) to 5 (high impact), rate the opportunities you have listed:

List and Rate the Opportunities	1	2	3	4	5
1.					
2.					
3.					
4.					
5.					
6.					

Next, order the opportunities as you ranked them and describe the steps you can take (or entrust someone to take) to align the opportunity with your business objectives.

Opportunity #1
The actions I will take and by when:
1. _____
2. _____
3. _____

Opportunity #2
The actions I will take and by when:
1. _____
2. _____
3. _____

Opportunity #3
The actions I will take and by when:
1. _____
2. _____
3. _____

Opportunity #4
The actions I will take and by when:

1. _____
2. _____
3. _____

Opportunity #5
The actions I will take and by when:

1. _____
2. _____
3. _____

Opportunity #6
The actions I will take and by when:

1. _____
2. _____
3. _____

STEP 3: PLAN YOUR GROWTH TRACK

i. Define and communicate why fixing the challenges and assessing opportunities are important to you as the owner, to the business, and to each team member.

ii. Set growth goals for core processes and for new growth areas:
   - How much time and resources are committed to protecting and maintaining the core?
   - How much time and resources are committed to experimenting with new growth?
   - Can the two tracks be aligned? If not, it may suggest your business is not mature enough and that more time end resources need to be invested in maintaining and protecting the core.

iii. Build the growth plan, gather ideas from your team to fill in the gaps, and get stakeholder and team buy-in.

STEP 4: EXECUTE YOUR GROWTH PLAN

i. Determine and agree with your accountability partner (e.g., franchisor field coach) on what the scorecard and tracking metrics will look like.

ii. Assign resources, responsibilities, and accountabilities.

iii. Get the team confident with experimenting around the edges. Explain the process to the team and that they'll be trying some new things, assessing whether they are beneficial or not to the business, and that if they don't work out, that's okay. Everyone has learned something.

STEP 5: MEASURE PROGRESS REGULARLY

Hold progress update meetings with your team; examine root causes of that progress (people, processes, equipment, money).

i. Review successes with the team and articulate the lessons that were learned:
  - what worked well that should be repeated
  - what worked to a degree and could work better with more commitment

ii. Review mistakes and failed experiments, and articulate the lessons that were learned:
  - what didn't work, and why
  - what parts of process might be adjusted for a next attempt
  - what additional resources might be needed for a next attempt

iii. Celebrate successes and lessons learned

Doug Phillip on this: "The ones (TPFs) that love the win [have this attitude]: 'I'm going to make a decision, even if it's a mistake. I'm going to learn from that mistake and I'm going to go forward.'"

STEP 6: APPLY LESSONS LEARNED AND MAKE MID-COURSE CORRECTIONS

When an experiment is proven to have a beneficial effect on the business, make it a deliberate practice until it is seamlessly integrated into your core process, meaning it has been internalized and systematized by you and your team.

A big impediment to franchisees' progress toward the next level in their Growth Helix is that they prematurely shift focus to a newly implemented process. Here's what Don Elliott of Great Clips has to say about this:

> Narrow it down. Focus. Find one or two nuggets, grab that one thing or whatever, and then just lock in on that thing, and get that implemented in your business, and get it to be kind of a standard part of your business, part of your operations, and then grab the next one, and just keep adding and building your business from there. A shotgun approach [trying to implement too many new ideas at once] doesn't get you anywhere.

Don never loses sight of the core processes; instead, he finds ways to add to or further optimize that core. His philosophy is to stick to one or two things until it becomes an autopilot part of your core process, then move onto the learning and implementing the next important thing.

Moving from new learning to operational efficiency to operational excellence is what these six steps are all about. Once you have reached operational excellence with any new process, congratulations! You've just completed a full cycle rotation for your Growth Helix, and you're ready to begin the next one.

Build for the Next Level of Growth: Wash, Rinse, Repeat

Once you've achieved your current level's growth goals, you're now ready to embark on your journey through your next level of growth. To get started on this growth cycle, it's the same six-step process all over again, this time with more knowledge and operational strength.

Begin by first going back to remaining pain/opportunity points that you identified in step 2 of your last growth cycle, and assess to what degree the remaining ones are still relevant. Also, assess if any new ones have emerged that might change the priority ranking. Then, continue through the remaining steps.

The objective now is for you to apply and practice this six-step growth process so that it will become second nature for you. A natural by-product is that you'll also be helping your key staff build this critical skillset. The better they learn it, the more responsibility they can take on, which will free up some of your bandwidth to focus on loftier business and personal growth goals.

Progressing though your Growth Helix is not about climbing to the top, not about being the best. It's about focusing on incremental improvement to counter the force of stagnation: "He who stays in place, goes backwards!" It is the path to remaining in the Performance Zone, and to achieving and maintaining operational excellence.

In Closing

Growth is not a race. Some thought leaders have debated whether running a business is a series of sprints or a marathon. Races still have only one winner, though, so that's a lot of conscious or subconscious pressure that we put on ourselves, on top of the myriad of pressures that come with running a business.

Using the Growth Helix will enable you to approach running your business as a journey, from where you are now to where you want to be, in time, in lifestyle, in income, in whatever is important for you to realize as an entrepreneur.

You are traveling a path of continual evolution, where month by month you are gaining knowledge, experience, and the ability to accomplish more. The more growth cycles you successfully progress through, the higher your growth spiral gets, the stronger your core systems become, and the more opportunity and growth you can capitalize upon.

Journeys are adventures, wrought with great experiences and challenges. In your entrepreneurial journey, you get to figure out where you want to go, the speed that you go at, who you want to travel with, etc. As an existing franchisee or business owner, you're already an entrepreneurial traveler, so the challenge at hand is to figure out where you want to go from where you are now, and how you want to enjoy the journey along the way.

Now that you're aware of what a Growth Helix is, you can begin working on strengthening and refining it, continually. Awareness is the supercharger to accelerating through the growth journey—internal awareness of self, team, resources, and processes; external awareness of customer, marketplace, and emerging trends, both micro and macro.

For entrepreneurs, success is an ever-evolving journey, ascending like a coiled spring:

- Define what it is now
- Define what it is down the road
- "Today" is yesterday's "down the road." Top entrepreneurs are acutely focused on short-, mid- and long-term goals so that their "down the road" can be readily achieved.

Be sure to download the Growth Plan Workbook (at theunstoppablefranchisee.com), which is fillable, to complete your Growth Helix exercises and strategies. The workbook also contains the surveys and journal exercises, as well as additional resources.

**Garyism: "What do we have to give up
for the time being in order to get started,
or in order to get ahead?"**

THE GROWTH HELIX APPLIED TO DRIVER NO. 1:
Grow a Next-Level Mindset

AS EXPLAINED IN PART ONE, there are seven drivers that work in unison to grow a business to the next level. At the top of the list of essential skills or traits that franchisees and other types of business owners have is called an "open mindset" or "growth mindset." The growth mindset results from the interaction of all the drivers. Cynthia Keenan of Blo Blow Dry Bar says:

> Have an open mindset. Be receptive for learning, but follow the system. The people that I see that are successful are people who have that innate entrepreneurship, but also are open to direction because that's being part of a larger system. So you come into it having a lot of your own ideas of what you're trying to create, but you also have to be very willing to learn new things, and you have to have the ability to take direction, because I see a lot of people who will come in and they've had a lot of success in another kind of business and they think it's going to translate. Part of what you're buying into as a franchise is their system and you need to trust it and be open to it.

Let's unpack Cynthia's wisdom and see how it links with the seven drivers:

Points of Wisdom	Link to
Successful people have an innate entrepreneurial spirit or skillset or mindset.	Driver No. 1: Grow a Next-Level Mindset Driver No. 4: Grow Your People Driver No. 6: Grow Your Interdependence
As a franchisee, this entrepreneurial drive is complemented by being open to take direction because their business is part of an ecosystem that is designed for success.	Driver No. 3: Grow Your Operational Management Skills Driver No. 5: Master the System
The franchisee is an idea machine, and is willing to learn new things. So they are happy to change their mind, which is the opposite of having a fixed mindset, which is rigid and restricted by limited thinking and biases. This also applies to recognizing that past success in business will not necessarily translate into success in the franchisee's new business.	Driver No. 1: Grow a Next-Level Mindset Driver No. 2: Grow Your Awareness
The growth or open mindset is able to embrace and trust the system.	Driver No. 4: Grow Your People Driver No. 5: Master the System Driver No. 6: Grow Your Interdependence

....

Garyism: "I'd rather manage the pain of change than live in fear of the alternative of staying stuck where I am."

"The dictionary is the only place that success comes before work." ANONYMOUS

....

The Growth Mindset focuses on incremental and continual growth and change. "Growth" is not just business growth or financial growth. Business growth and financial growth are downstream by-products of growth in overcoming challenges in other areas first. It could be personal, operational, technological innovation, etc. In fact, a significant component of growth is knowledge growth and skills growth, as Cynthia Keenan points out.

- Knowledge growth happens when we acquire and understand additional information.
- Skills growth happens only when we effectively apply that new knowledge.
- Skills mastery comes much later, after many hours of purposeful practice.

Complete the following exercise on next-level mindset in your Growth Plan Workbook. Reread Cynthia Keenan's take on a next-level mindset. What pain points might you be experiencing in the area between following the system and wanting to innovate? Between learning and trying new things while taking direction? List and rate the pain points that are affecting your business growth and preventing you from achieving business objectives.

List and Rate the Pain Points	1	2	3	4	5
1.					
2.					
3.					
4.					
5.					
6.					

Next, prioritize the pain points and describe the steps you can take to break the challenge into manageable and solvable steps.

Now, what opportunities have you come to see by applying your learning muscle? What improvements have you applied that are contributing to business growth? On a scale of 1 (low impact) to 5 (high impact), list and rate the opportunities that can contribute and are contributing to business growth:

List and Rate the Opportunities	1	2	3	4	5
1.					
2.					
3.					
4.					
5.					
6.					

Next, prioritize the opportunities and describe the steps you can take to break them into actionable steps.

In Closing

When I meet top-performing franchisees, I'm always curious about what their goals are. They love to talk about where they are growing, and sometimes it has little to do with their business. It could be taking up a new sport or hobby, soaking up cultures of distant lands through travel, or taking up a new language.

The common denominator to learning of any kind is that you are increasing your awareness about something. Taking up a sport or hobby brings awareness of a new skillset; travel brings awareness of a new environment; learning a new language combines awareness of communication, history and culture.

Awareness has everything to do with running a successful business. How to identify and prioritize which area to focus on is one of the most important aspects of TPFs' success. It is the exemplification of growing their management and leadership skills.

In the words of one of the founding grandfathers of our franchise industry, Ray Kroc: "Are you green and growing or ripe and rotting?"

THE GROWTH HELIX APPLIED TO DRIVER NO. 2:
Grow Your Awareness

WE ARE CREATURES OF our environment, and we respond and interact with that environment every day, both consciously and subconsciously. Whether we bought our franchise, started our business from scratch, or bought an existing business, we, in essence, chose to live, work, and lead in that environment.

Our job as a business owner, leader, and manager is to learn and understand the many conditions of our current environment, including their causes and impacts. Going back to what Cynthia Keenan says, how open a channel are you for new ideas?

Once we start paying attention to what these conditions are trying to tell us—whether painful or pleasurable—we create space so that the answers and solutions can come into our awareness.

Ned Lyerly, chief executive officer of Hardee's and Carl's Jr., talks about the importance of awareness: "I think the people skills that I see in successful franchisees are just very special. And the successful franchisees have awareness in how they interact in all their environments."

Being able to see and hear these new answers and solutions requires having an open mind, a reporter's curiosity, a thirst for the truth through seeking multiple perspectives. It's a willingness to accept that other people's points of view or ways of doing things might be more effective than yours. Many franchisees I interviewed said they did not want to be or be seen as the smartest person in the room.

It starts with being willing to acknowledge that your business has performance gap areas, as do you. This opens the door to the prospect of embracing new possibilities, to be willing to change some things, and evolve incrementally. It also starts with accepting that what got you to your current level of performance will not guarantee your ability to achieve your next level, or even guarantee that you can maintain your current level.

"What got you here won't get you there!"

Marshall Goldsmith wrote a great book by this name for corporate leaders; his words are just as true for franchisees and small business owners.

All the sacrifice, time, effort, and money expended to get you to your current level of success will not get you to the next level of success. Markets change, conditions change, and the COVID-19 pandemic reshaped how we live, work and play. If you want to get to your next level at some element of your business, you'll need to increase your proficiency in some of the skills and abilities you possess, develop new ones, and be clear-minded about seeing the value in new perspectives. So, we come back to the importance and relevance of your growth catalysts. In the exercise below, list your pain points and opportunities as they apply to the driver of awareness. Identifying and solving problems and taking steps to make the most of opportunities are examples of growth catalysts.

Walter Bond, a famous professional basketball player, says it this way: "The next level is a lifestyle; the next level is a tangible place. You are in charge of your next level. If you want to get to your next level, you can, but you must become someone different!"[21]

Bond has a vision, as do entrepreneurs. To achieve that vision means evolving and not standing still. Getting to a next level requires a focused effort on acquiring new knowledge and skills so that you can change certain behaviors. As a pro athlete, Bond made minor but consistent shifts of focus and effort on a few critically important things that upgraded his performance.

So, what are the few critically important things that awareness has identified for you to grow your business?

First, what are your awareness pain points that are affecting your business growth? On a scale of 1 (low impact) to 5 (high impact), list and rate the pain points:

List and Rate the Pain Points	1	2	3	4	5
1.					
2.					
3.					
4.					
5.					
6.					

Next, prioritize the pain points and describe the steps you can take to break the challenge into manageable and solvable steps.

Second, what opportunities have you come to see by applying awareness? On a scale of 1 (low impact) to 5 (high impact), list and rate the opportunities that can contribute to business growth:

List and Rate the Opportunities	1	2	3	4	5
1.					
2.					
3.					
4.					
5.					
6.					

Next, prioritize the opportunities and describe the steps you can take to break them into actionable steps.

In Closing

I will close this section with the words of Vanessa Yakobson, CEO of Blo Blow Dry Bar:

> As you evolve with a franchise system, particularly if you evolve to become a multi-unit owner, you've got to figure out how to do things differently. Because we know in business that businesses that rest on their laurels, and don't update their systems and don't anticipate where change is going to come from, are the ones that fail.

THE GROWTH HELIX APPLIED TO DRIVER NO. 3:
Grow Your Operational Management Skills

OPERATIONAL MANAGEMENT is tightly linked to the core processes of the Growth Helix. Remember, this is what you do that works every day, every week, and every month. You are following the franchisor's model and executing to the best of your ability. Doing so has sustained your business and reached a level that you might be happy with, but overall you want to do better.

Wanting to do better is likely leading you to ask questions about the franchisor's model and its processes. Could anything be done a bit differently that would create an efficiency that saves time and money? What experimentation could you do to test your ideas? This notion is captured in Graham Weihmiller's quote from chapter 4:

> Top performers are really execution focused ... The franchisee that is focused on execution of the existing brand is probably going to do better. Now, they should always provide ideas and feedback to the franchisor, and the franchisor ideally is going to involve them in the decision-making process. But I think what is key is that the franchisee understands at any given point, their primary role is the excellent and consistent execution of the existing model.

Graham is warning the new franchisee not to run before they can walk. Growing the business requires growing a next-level mindset (Driver No. 1) and growing your awareness (Driver No. 2). Sound operational management depends on having the right mindset and constantly reading the signs around you to make the right decisions about how you are running the business. It is about being execution focused.

The success of your business rests on optimally managing the drivers of your business. It takes self-awareness to say "I am not managing this driver as well as I should be, so I need to take action to close the gap." The same awareness extends to every member of your team. Where are proficiencies lacking?

In the exercise below, list your pain points and opportunities as they apply to the driver of operational management. Identifying and solving problems and taking steps to make the most of opportunities are examples of growth catalysts. You may use the seven areas of operational management we discussed as a guide:

- customer acquisition (marketing and sales)
- production
- delivery/fulfillment
- human resources/staffing
- financial management
- facilities and equipment maintenance
- safety and security

First, what are your operational management pain points that are affecting your business stability and growth? On a scale of 1 (low impact) to 5 (high impact), list and rate the pain points:

List and Rate the Pain Points	1	2	3	4	5
1.					
2.					
3.					
4.					
5.					
6.					

Next, prioritize the pain points and describe the steps you can take to break the challenge into manageable and solvable steps.

Second, what opportunities have you come to see by assessing the status of your operational management? On a scale of 1 (low impact) to 5 (high impact), list and rate the opportunities that can contribute to business growth:

List and Rate the Opportunities	1	2	3	4	5
1.					
2.					
3.					
4.					
5.					
6.					

Next, prioritize the opportunities and describe the steps you can take to break them into actionable steps.

In Closing

Sam Reges, a very successful franchisee with Great Clips, believes in experimentation. In our interview, she explained:

> I think that it's important to know that you're going to fail, and frankly, when you fail, that's how you build wherever you're going to build next. Unfortunately, sometimes those things come too late, and then you have to rebuild more than you would have had to maybe if it had been caught sooner. But you don't know until you know.
>
> I think that you do have to experience that idea of, "Well, we tried this and it did not go well, and where do we go from here?" For me, it's asking "Where do we go from here?" that I think makes you the most honest in your interactions with your staff. You are saying, "You know what? We're going to try this. You guys are scared, and so are we, and we're going to try this. If it doesn't work, we're going to admit that it doesn't work and we're going to figure out where to go next."

And Dan Monaghan's wisdom takes this idea further:

> We find that some of the highest performers are people that are bringing new ideas to the table. Because you could have the best franchise system in the world, it could be bulletproof, but all of a sudden two months from now it's no longer what it was because the world changed, the market changed, the competition changed, technology changed.

The Growth Helix permits experimentation. Experimentation is essential for learning, which is a core leadership skill.

THE GROWTH HELIX APPLIED TO DRIVER NO. 4:
Grow Your People

ONE OF THE KEY POINTS to be understood is how management and leadership are different. They are both highly skilled roles, but require different attributes. That is one of the reasons I have devoted a chapter to each topic. Recall what Angela Brown says about leadership: "Leadership is next level—it's where you inspire people to do things they never thought were possible. It takes a little bit of extra effort and time on your part as a leader, but it's so rewarding. You have to be intentional—you can't wing it. Every conversation with every client, and every team member, matters."

The consistent execution of the franchisor's existing model requires management skills and leadership to work in tandem. Leadership is the gateway to:

1. building the right culture based on the brand's values and the leader's values
2. a curiosity mindset that inspires learning and development among the team
3. setting the team up for success
4. attracting talent because you are role modeling empathy, accountability, respect, inclusion, and the need to have fun—in other words, you define servant leadership

Let's bring servant leadership into focus as it applies to the four critical areas of leadership as a driver of your business. In the exercise below, list your pain points and opportunities as they apply to how you lead. Use the following questions as a guide to assess your pain points and opportunities as you reflect on how your leadership style is showing up through your employees:

- What is driving or preventing consistent customer wins? Where is my leadership style contributing or falling short regarding delivering optimum customer experiences through my team?
- What is the cause of employee complaints? Are those causes or symptoms of a bigger issue? Who might be feeling that they are not an integral part of my team?
- To what degree have I built a high-trust culture? How might this relate to the Performance Zone quadrant I am operating in?
- What needs to shift?

List the leadership pain points that are challenging running your business well. On a scale of 1 (low impact) to 5 (high impact), list and rate the pain points:

List and Rate the Pain Points	1	2	3	4	5
1.					
2.					
3.					
4.					
5.					
6.					

Next, prioritize the pain points and describe the steps you can take to break the challenge into manageable and solvable steps.

Now, consider what opportunities have come to light in assessing your leadership skills and attributes. On a scale of 1 (low impact) to 5 (high impact), list and rate the opportunities that can contribute to business growth. Use the following questions as a guide to assess how your leadership is proving effective if any of these scenarios apply: "How is my leadership style..."

- contributing to higher customer retention and growing revenues? What more can I do to increase my customer base?
- contributing to the success, safety, and happiness of my employees? What more can I do for them to improve their work/life balance or make them feel more invested in the brand?
- contributing to my ability to work and lead at a high level consistently? What more can I do to invest in my leadership capacity?

List and Rate the Opportunities	1	2	3	4	5
1.					
2.					
3.					
4.					
5.					
6.					

Next, prioritize the opportunities and describe the steps you can take to break them into actionable steps.

In Closing

It is worth repeating that what my research revealed about top performers is that while they certainly practice servant leadership, where they win is by first looking after others in their orbit. The evidence is that by looking after others first, their business is stronger and more profitable than others that don't put their people first. Strong teams keep the business running, even when the owner isn't around; develop rich relationships with customers and staff; and team members live richer, more fulfilling personal lives.

Near the end of chapter 5, I included an excerpt from my interview with Emily Wilcox, a very successful franchisee with Great Clips. She spoke about engaging with employees and the importance of communication:

> Developing your people is a critical aspect—making sure that they know what's expected of them. Don't assume that they know what something is. Help and guide them, so they know how to perform well in their role. So we spend a lot of time developing our stylists, our leaders. We're very actively involved in that from the day that somebody's hired. It's a critical piece of who we are.
>
> And, I think, communication. I mean, our employees hear from me. They see me. They hear from me, whether it's on Facebook or my voice on the phone. They're going to see me in the salons. I probably over-communicate, using as many avenues to communicate as possible. Knowledge is power, and the more that people know, the more that they're able to effectively do their job.

In case you need more convincing, remember what Charles Bonfiglio, CEO of Tint World, has to say on empowerment:

> I think the top skillset for a leader, regardless of how qualified someone is in sales, operations, or the technical aspects, is being able to empower their employees to do a good job and own their position. The franchisee can work on the business and not need to be in it every day, because they're empowering leaders within their

business system, and that allows them to grow more units with more staff who take care of the customer in the same way as if they were there.

Emily and Charles are classic examples of leaders that empower others. Notice how present Emily is as a leader. Notice how she invests in training and development. When her team is effective in their role, the indisputable result is that the customer wins. Emily has ten salons—I'd say that is a winning formula. Charles's formula is also focused on satisfied customers by building leadership skills in the team. Again, the message is the same—empower your people.

THE GROWTH HELIX APPLIED TO DRIVER NO. 5:
Master the System

HAVE NO ILLUSIONS ABOUT the amount of hard work that is required in launching any business, including a franchise. Every franchisee must go through a learning journey fraught with challenges, adversity, pain, and excitement—and a good mix of wins and losses. In other words, they have to *do*. They have to learn, make mistakes, grow, and evolve into becoming a successful business owner. Much of that learning is about understanding a system and its operational drivers. For that learning, franchisees must draw upon the knowledge and experience of their franchisor's leadership team and other successful franchisees within their system.

Josh Skolnick, CEO of HorsePower Brands, talks about how he emphasizes the work element to new franchisees: "Starting a new business, if you make the commitment to work harder than you've ever worked in your life for the next twenty-four months, put more into this in the next twenty-four months than anything you've ever done in your life, you're going to get yourself to a place where the return on investment and return on time will be second to none."

But Josh then has a warning. In his experience, he says, "And everybody's willing to do that up-front, but actions speak louder than words. And then you'd be surprised, once they get in, there's always an excuse, something in the way of why they didn't do it. I always call the excuses the should haves, could haves, would haves—*we should have invested in this, we would have invested in this, or we could have invested in this*—but there's always objections as to why they didn't."

Breaking down the growth journey into three steps enables the franchisee to identify stuck points and find a solution. These three steps are:

Phase 1: Learning the system

Phase 2: Knowing the system

Phase 3: Mastering the system

In the exercise below, list your pain points and opportunities as they apply to the driver of mastering the system. Identifying and solving problems and taking steps to make the most of opportunities are examples of growth catalysts. You may use the three phases of the growth journey as a guide.

First, what are the "mastering the system pain points" that are affecting your growth journey? If you are in the first two-year phase (learning the system), where might you be stuck? In this stage, you are taking in information at a blistering pace. You are getting operations up and running, dealing with hiring and training, financial management, marketing and sales. Think about these aspects as you list your first-phase pain points.

If you are in the second phase (knowing the system), where might you be stuck? Recall that in the second phase you are operating from a place of some accumulated and internalized knowledge, while recognizing that there's still a lot of learning in store and much growing yet to be done. A key indicator that you have moved into the Knowing the System phase is that you no longer have to think about how to execute on certain aspects of the business. You are developing as a leader and your team is showing greater proficiency. You are focused on improving cash flow and increasing revenue. Are you committing your people, time, and money resources optimally? Have you got your KPIs in place? What are the data telling you? Think about these aspects as you list your second-phase pain points.

If you are in the third phase (mastering the system), where might you be stuck? In this phase, the learning journey evolves to mastering operational excellence, while also driving scalability. In order to achieve next-level growth, new market opportunities have to be identified and pursued; new choke points emerge and have to be resolved; and TPFs focus on attacking those opportunities and choke points with disciplined and progressive learning so that they can quickly adjust. Is your team fully built and highly trained? Are goals and objectives being met on time? Is your leadership style creating the right culture for the team to thrive and take on more responsibility? Is everyone a brand ambassador? Think about these aspects as you list your third-phase pain points.

On a scale of 1 (low impact) to 5 (high impact), list and rate the pain points:

List and Rate the Pain Points	1	2	3	4	5
1.					
2.					
3.					
4.					
5.					
6.					

Next, prioritize the pain points and describe the steps you can take to break the challenge into manageable and solvable steps.

Now, what opportunities have you come to see by assessing the status of your system mastery? For example, where have you discovered process efficiencies that reduce time and cost? Who among your team shows promise for accelerated development? What interactions with customers have given you ideas as to how improve the business? Which KPIs are robust, and which may be unhelpful and not worth your attention? On a scale of 1 (low impact) to 5 (high impact), list and rate the opportunities that can contribute to business growth:

List and Rate the Opportunities	1	2	3	4	5
1.					
2.					
3.					
4.					
5.					
6.					

Next, prioritize the opportunities and describe the steps you can take to break them into actionable steps.

In Closing

As the franchisee comes ever closer to mastering the system (although it is always a work in progress), they become beacons of performance and excellence that newer franchisees seek to emulate; they are the thought leaders of the franchise system. They are highly active and involved, both in their own businesses and in finding ways to strengthen the brand and system. They have earned a place at the franchisor's strategy table because they have evolved to a point where they see the greatest path to success is to put the franchise system's interests ahead of their own. Their mindset is "Together, we win more": more market share, more operating margin, more happiness and satisfaction, more frequently!

Jason Zickerman maintains there is a status attached to being a top performer: "Top performers want to be acknowledged as top performers. Top performers want to be put in the position where they are with other top performers. Being part of that club. But they want to be in that group of excellence not because they want the label of the club, but because they are excited by the idea that they could learn from other people who are excellent."

THE GROWTH HELIX APPLIED TO DRIVER NO. 6:
Grow Your Interdependence

THIS SIXTH DRIVER is about growing your interdependence, which is the sign of a maturing and successful business. As you'll recall from chapter 7, I liken the process to the stages of childhood, teenagerhood, and adulthood.

So let's look at this parallel maturity journey that franchisees must travel as they ramp up their business, achieve stability, and eventually reach the point where their business achieves a level of performance that is reflective of the franchisee's hard work and the degree to which they and their franchisor support team have come together.

The franchisor, instead of exhibiting a type of controlling behavior through initial training, early coaching, and ongoing development, strives to guide the new franchisee's learning curve and influence behaviors in order to build desirable habits that focus on following the system.

It's in the later stages of relationship maturity when the franchisee has the opportunity to derive the greatest value and benefit of the franchise system. And part of this maturation journey requires that franchisees must be open to learning and doing things as prescribed by the franchisor, because seldom is a system or process static.

What do these behaviors look like in the eyes of a very successful franchise CEO? Catherine Monson, CEO of Propelled Brands, believes that poor performance is caused by not paying attention to the foundation the franchisor has laid and not following the franchise brand's operating model, and that it is imperative to get the franchisee back on track:

> I believe the five common characteristics of all highly successful people are positive mental attitude, goal-directed behavior, self-motivation, a sense of urgency, and never stopping learning. So I think these are foundational success factors.
>
> These are the factors that separate the franchisees with consistent sales growth and consistent profit growth from the lesser performers. It's really easy to identify the reasons for having a weak franchise. They're not developing and empowering their people. They're not delegating. They're not focused on the key KPIs. They are their own logjam or bandwidth challenge.

These foundational success factors strongly influence the amount of revenue and knowledge share delivered by top franchisees.

Interdependent franchisees are committed to constant growth and high levels of achievement. They derive maximum value from the brand, from the systems, and from the franchisor's knowledge and resources. They seek out and actively engage with other top franchisees, and challenge each other to excel even further. They are consistently found in the top 25 percent of the franchisee performance bell curve, and are among the happiest and most successful franchisees in the entire system.

As you'll recall from chapter 7, the significance of transitioning from the independent stage to the interdependent stage was one of the most important things that evolved from my research. Without exception, every single top-performing franchisee demonstrated and espoused the mindset and all the qualities of having an inter-dependent relationship with their franchisor.

In the exercise below, list your pain points and opportunities as they apply to the driver of growing your interdependence. Identi-fying and solving problems and taking steps to make the most of opportunities are examples of growth catalysts.

First, what are the growing your interdependence pain points that are affecting your business growth? For example, is your rela-tionship with the franchisor maturing at a pace that aligns with the pace of your business development? Do you require less hands-on help and more strategic planning? What is getting in the way of scaling your business and making it sustainable? On a scale of 1 (low impact) to 5 (high impact), list and rate the pain points:

List and Rate the Pain Points	1	2	3	4	5
1.					
2.					
3.					
4.					
5.					
6.					

Next, prioritize the pain points and describe the steps you can take to break the challenge into manageable and solvable steps.

Now, what opportunities have you come to see as you have grown your interdependence? For example, how has your leadership style changed? The relationship with the community you serve? Are there unexpected markets you are tapping into? Are you making the most effective use of the collective brain trust? What new ideas are percolating that can help your brand outperform your competi-tors? On a scale of 1 (low impact) to 5 (high impact), list and rate the opportunities that can contribute to business growth:

List and Rate the Opportunities	1	2	3	4	5
1.					
2.					
3.					
4.					
5.					
6.					

Next, prioritize the opportunities and describe the steps you can take to break them into actionable SMART goal steps (Specific, Measurable, Achievable, Realistic, and Time-bound).

In Closing

Colin Bates, a regional developer with Jan-Pro, says there is no end point to interdependence. To think you've arrived at such a point is going to stultify your business. He says,

> Getting to the next level is what counts. Don't even accept the next level as the end-all be-all. That's the beginning of the next iteration beyond that. I constantly challenge my people for scalable, sustainable processes. We're going to grow this business. In everything that you do in a day, ask yourself, "Is this the best, most efficient, most effective way that we can do this? Or are we doing it this way because it fits our needs today, as opposed to looking at what we need to do in the future?"

What "must get done" in the future is the hallmark thinking of a great leader. This point is so important to the Growth Helix that I want to repeat these words from Dan Monaghan:

> In franchising, we have this network effect, where a franchise system with fifty franchisees or one hundred learns so much faster.

Our only competitive advantage in today's world is the speed at which we learn. And if the franchisor is wired correctly, it becomes a learning organization. Which means that they're constantly on the lookout for the innovations that are happening in the system.

And in this world, the power comes from everyone sharing. Because that gives us competitive advantage if we're moving faster than our competitors and if we're learning faster than our competitors. And so, a new idea could emerge anywhere within the system. What that means is you're going to constantly be getting new ideas and the system's going to constantly be evolving. But you also have to be a contributor to that. And everyone has different strengths and weaknesses, and things they bring to the table. But that is an important success trait, you're willing to share.

THE GROWTH HELIX APPLIED TO DRIVER NO. 7:
Cultivate the Neural Network of Your Business

ASK YOUR FRANCHISOR to help you get a better handle on which KPIs are the most critical, and for some direction on how to access and understand this information. As you get more adept with leveraging KPI data, then you can take things to the next level by having more robust discussions with the TPFs in your system about which KPIs they pay close attention to, and more importantly, how they use this information to guide their decisions.

In the exercise below, list your pain points and opportunities as they apply to the driver of measuring success. Identifying and solving problems and taking steps to make the most of opportunities are examples of growth catalysts.

First, what are your pain points around KPIs and their application? For example, have you identified the KPIs that provide you with the right data and quality of data that can pinpoint the performance of your business? When you step back and take a high-level view of the data, are information gaps showing up? On a scale of 1 (low impact) to 5 (high impact), list and rate the pain points:

List and Rate the Pain Points	1	2	3	4	5
1.					
2.					
3.					
4.					
5.					
6.					

Next, prioritize the pain points and describe the steps you can take to break the challenge into manageable and solvable steps.

Now, what opportunities have you come to see as you use and refine your KPIs? For example, how might have KPIs changed the way you manage your numbers, train your team, or interact with customers? Have KPIs provided insights into your business that have generated new ideas and innovations? On a scale of 1 (low impact) to 5 (high impact), list and rate the opportunities that can contribute to business growth through measuring success:

List and Rate the Opportunities	1	2	3	4	5
1.					
2.					
3.					
4.					
5.					
6.					

Next, prioritize the opportunities and describe the steps you can take to break them into actionable steps.

In Closing

I want to restate this because it's so important: If you aren't using a robust KPI measurement process, then *implementing use of KPIs or improving on how you're presently using KPIs is the single most important next step you can take to start improving your business,* because every other operational improvement you will want to make will stem from better measurement of your KPI. Why? Because the KPI inform all of my other six drivers. Let's revisit the self-fulfilling prophecy feedback loop:

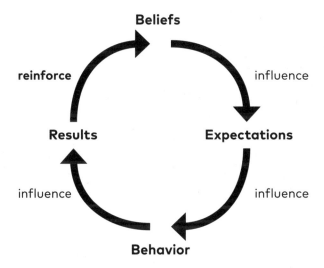

Think about how a few vital KPIs can affect every part of this loop, and enable you to make faster, better, more informed decisions. Recall all of the TPFs I interviewed for this book; the nature of their businesses is not dissimilar to yours. TPFs dictated the degree of complexity of the available data that enabled them to "know their numbers," but every one of the TPFs had clarity on the critical numbers that mattered in their business; more importantly, every one of them looked at and leveraged that data at least weekly, and in some cases daily.

When norm-based KPI data is available (e.g., system-average performance ratios like sales conversion rations, production time, or food costs), the importance of having some goals focused on achieving or beating those ratios helps the business to progress to higher levels operational excellence. As Peter Drucker famously said, "A strategy without metrics is just a wish. And metrics that are not aligned with strategic objectives are a waste of time."

As we shared in chapter 5, which covered leadership, communicating goals and objectives to your team and directing them towards taking hyper-focused action are critical parts of success. Being able to measure that performance and communicate progress back to your team is one thing; remember that the quality of that communication is only as good as the quality of the KPI data you're using.

If using KPIs is the single most important next step you can take to start improving your business, you might be asking why I've chosen to place KPIs and measuring success as the last of the seven drivers. I did so because, for most new franchisees, learning and measuring KPIs is a new skill that has to be developed; it is often misunderstood, and it can be intimidating. One of the reasons is that during the launch phase, a new franchisee is naturally underperforming against system averages. In addition, they are so busy learning all the other aspects of how to run their new business, the available time to learn this new skill is limited.

AFTERWORD

I WILL LEAVE YOU with a final word from Angela Brown and then present three of my own philosophies that I've been living for years. First, Angela:

> You can't put a price tag on having a forum of people who can educate you on the fundamentals of the business and the mindset it takes to be successful, which I think is the most important part of success. It is the mindset that you choose to approach your business every day. I want to be around the people who have the mindset of winning, overcoming, and feeling accomplished.

MY PHILOSOPHIES:
"Work smart. Play well."
Playing hard takes too much of a toll on the brain and the body; working hard without observing the lessons from the mistakes and from the wins squanders energy and focus. When you build your aware-sense to the point where you can see in real time the lessons from your successes and failures alike, and apply those in your ongoing business activities, that's working smart! It also means being unstoppable. It means strengthening your next-level mindset and using aware-sense to constantly know where to focus your energy and your primary resources. And doing that empowers you

to "play well"—to make time for the things outside of your business that you want to experience.

"Seize the day."
"On the plains of hesitation lie the blackened bones of countless millions who, at the dawn of victory lay down to rest, and in resting, died." This quote from Adlai Stevenson has always spoken to me about the importance of seizing the day. In my first-responder days I saw how precious life is. Whatever your dreams, goals, and ambitions are, don't "lay down to rest." Yes, take enough time to recharge, but do not fall into the trap of getting too comfortable and staying there too long. Do something, every day, to take at least one next step in this life journey you're on, and make sure to find enjoyment in enough of your steps!

"I believe in you."
My final closing philosophy is that the most powerful combined words in the English language are *I believe in you*.

Are these words not what we wanted to hear from our parents when we were young, from our bosses in our early career, and from our personal relationship partners? Are they not what your team members want to hear from you, through words, or better yet through your actions?

You might be reacting to this statement regarding a specific person on your team by thinking "but I don't believe in_____." Far more importantly, when you look at yourself in the mirror—and that's the ultimate measure, isn't it?—it's easier to say "I believe in you" when things are going well, but it's way more difficult when you're amidst a maelstrom of challenges.

If you find yourself not believing in yourself, or in someone on your team, or maybe in your relationship with your franchisor, then here's a path from doubt and skepticism about changing the relationship dynamic with that person: add the word "enough."

I believe in you *enough* that I'm confident you are ready and willing to apply several concepts and ideas from this book in your business. You wouldn't have picked up this book if you weren't motivated to make a shift somewhere to realize next-level growth. I believe in you enough to be sure that you'll grab your next power-up and commit to applying it, then come back to this book again to grab another power-up. Wash, rinse, repeat.

THANK YOU FOR READING MY BOOK. Please contact me. I am happy to learn about your ideas, challenges and opportunities. And I will value your feedback on which parts of this book have empowered you to achieve your next level, and to write your own unstoppable journey. As you begin the next season of your franchise journey, I wish you much success with your enterprise.

CONGRATULATIONS ON UNDERTAKING YOUR JOURNEY TO BECOMING UNSTOPPABLE!

To help you implement what you've learned in these pages, use this QR code to access my fillable PDF workbook. In it, you'll find every exercise and survey in *The Unstoppable Franchisee.*

The beauty of the workbook is that it meets you where you are and enables you to "start with the soil" as you begin the next "season" of your business. Once you've achieved greater proficiency in your first area of need, you can come back to this workbook to tackle the next driver, and then the next, and the next . . .

Kickstart your transformation to becoming unstoppable; scan the QR code to accelerate transformational, next-level growth in your business!

Acknowledgments

AN OFT-USED PHRASE in franchising is that "you're in business for yourself, but not by yourself"—which is evidence of just how highly collaborative a successful franchise business is. This book is no different. It's not possible to include the vast number of contributors to this book; to those of you who don't get mentioned personally here, know that I'm deeply grateful for the wisdom you've shared with me along the way.

It's my privilege to call out and thank the following:

To the 2,000-plus clients of my FranNet franchise whom I and my team have had the opportunity to guide through your franchise ownership search journey; your time with us helped us to better understand and appreciate the many personal and professional catalysts for transitioning from corporate to self-employment. Thank you for your trust. The seeds of inspiration for this book came from watching you launch and grow your franchises.

Thank you to all the top franchisees and to all the franchisor presidents, CEOs, and senior executives who actively participated in my research and who gave selflessly of their time and wisdom for my interviews. (See the complete list on pages ix–x.) Collectively, you helped me look at success drivers and detractors from multiple lenses in a wide range of industries. Words cannot capture the immense gratitude I have for your contribution, for without it this book would not have been possible.

To Don Loney, editor extraordinaire, writing coach, mentor, and friend. Don, from the very start you understood my vision and purpose for this book. You constantly listened, questioned, and refined my thinking. By shining light into the dark, underdeveloped corners of the content, you challenged my findings and enabled me to shape the concepts here into this finished work. I'm forever grateful for you bringing to bear your thought leadership, knowledge, and experience. I look forward to doing more great work together!

Thank you to Chris Labonté and the whole team at Figure 1 Publishing for the laborious work involved to bring this book from manuscript to market. A special thanks to Steve Cameron for countless hours reviewing each manuscript version and further refining the book to improve the reader's experience.

To my mom and dad for loving me and supporting me unconditionally.

To my kids, Mike and Marie-Claire; watching you grow, mature, and follow your passions continues to make me a proud dad.

To Lindsay, my best friend, my inspiration, and my travelling partner on this journey called life. You have always supported me in whatever ventures I undertake. This project, however, was unlike any other; you listened and challenged my ideas, redirected my focus when needed, and gave me the space required to complete this project. Little did either of us know that it would take nearly two years of early mornings, long nights, and weekends. Like everything else, you were there every step of the way. Without you at my side and in my heart, this book would have never made it to market; I'm eternally grateful for having you in my life.

GARY PRENEVOST, *November 2022*

Notes

I provide sources below for pertinent details. Publicly spoken words and famous attributions and the like are widely available and as such are not cited here unless deemed worthwhile for providing additional context. The vast majority of the quotes found in the book are from interviews I conducted.

1. In her additional role as Director of Veterans Affairs for Neighborly, Thompson is responsible for engaging with veterans and securing positions in its franchises.
2. Jim Collins, *Good to Great: Why Some Companies Make the Leap... and Others Don't.* New York: HarperCollins, 2001, 11.
3. surfhungry.com/how-much-do-pro-surfers-make, accessed November 26, 2021.
4. thesaltsirens.com/how-much-money-do-surfers-make, accessed November 26, 2021.
5. Carol Dweck, "What Having a 'Growth Mindset' Actually Means." *Harvard Business Review* (January 13, 2016). hbr.org/ 2016/01/ what-having-a-growth-mindset-actually-means.
6. Mindsets.com, accessed October 8, 2021.
7. Carol Dweck, hbr.org/ 2016/01/what-having-a-growth-mindset-actually-means.
8. Mindsets.com, accessed October 8, 2021.

9. Simon Sinek, "Two Ways to See the World," https://www.linked in.com/feed/update/urn:li:activity:67344544381545512 96/.

10. Les Stroud, "Survivorman Les Stroud Answers Survival Questions from Twitter," https://www.youtube.com/ watch?v=hblks-lQhVo'.

11. Robert K. Merton, *The Antioch Review*, Vol. 8, No. 2 (Summer, 1948), pp. 193–210.

12. Enrique Rubio, "The Evolving Mindset," July 2015. linkedin. com/pulse/evolving-mindset-enrique-rubio, accessed May 30, 2022.

13. Rory Vaden, *Take the Stairs: 7 Steps to Achieving True Success*. New York: Penguin, 2002.

14. rethinksurvival.com/employing-les-strouds-3-zones-of-assessment, accessed March 31, 2022.

15. Corporatefinanceinstitute.com/resources/careers/soft-skills/management-skills, accessed March 20, 2022.

16. barrypopik.com/index.php/new_york_city/entry/nothing_happens_until_someone_sells_something, accessed March 20, 2022.

17. Also see Robert K. Greenleaf, *Servant Leadership: A Journey into the Nature of Legitimate Power and Greatness*. Mahwah, NJ: Paulist Press, 2002.

18. Daniel H. Pink, *Drive: The Surprising Truth about What Motivates Us*. New York: Penguin, 2011.

19. motivationworks.com/white-paper-the-critical-missing-piece-from-your-employee-engagement-efforts, accessed May 27, 2022.

20. https://kpi.org/KPI-Basics, accessed May 27, 2022. © 2022 KPI. org and Balanced Scorecard Institute, both Strategy Management Group companies. Used with permission.

21. https://www.youtube.com/watch?v=0DJDLW6Mlo8&t=10s, accessed October 17, 2021.

Index

About the Author

GARY PRENEVOST is a thirty-year franchise veteran and is one of North America's top franchise consultants. As a passionate entrepreneur and lifelong learner, Prenevost is a calculated risk-taker who thrives on creating opportunities for others, constantly redefining his comfort zone while helping others push the limits of what they thought possible. Prenevost has bought single, multi-unit, and master franchises for himself; brought American franchise concepts to Canada; helped independent businesses become franchisors; and coached hundreds of entrepreneurs. Currently, Prenevost is a multi-unit franchise owner with FranNet, where he and his team have helped over 2,000 prospective franchisee clients fully explore their franchise ownership options. *The Unstoppable Franchisee* is Prenevost's first book.